Crony Capitalism and Economic Growth in Latin America

Edited by **Stephen Haber**

Crony Capitalism and Economic Growth in Latin America
Theory and Evidence

Hoover Institution Press Stanford University Stanford, California www.hoover.org

Hoover Institution Press Publication No. 488

First printing 2002
07 06 05 04 03 02   9 8 7 6 5 4 3 2 1

Manufactured in the United States of America

The paper used in this publication meets the minimum requirements
of American National Standard for Information Sciences—Permanence
of Paper for Printed Library Materials, ANSI Z39.48–1984. ⊗

Library of Congress Cataloging-in-Publication Data

Crony capitalism and economic growth in Latin America : theory and
evidence / edited by Stephen Haber.
        p.   cm.
  Based on a conference organized by the Hoover Institution in
Puebla, Mexico in 1999.
  Includes bibliographical references and index.
  ISBN 0-8179-9962-0
  1. Latin America—Economic policy—Congresses. 2. Political
corruption—Economic aspects—Latin America—Congresses.
3. Capitalism—Latin America—Congresses. I. Haber, Stephen H., 1957–
II. Hoover Institution on War, Revolution and Peace.
HC125 .C798 2002
338.98—dc21   2001044358

Contents

Acknowledgments

This volume is the product of a symposium organized by the Hoover Institution in 1999. That symposium took place as part of the Congreso de las Américas, which was organized and hosted by the Universidad de las Américas, in Puebla, Mexico. We would like to thank Enrique Cárdenas, rector of the Universidad de las Américas, for organizing the Congreso de las Américas and for serving as a genial host to the group from Hoover. Major financial support for the symposium and this volume was provided by the Hoover Institution. We would like to express our thanks to John Raisian, director of the Hoover Institution. We are also in debt to John Raisian and the broader community of Hoover scholars for creating a venue in which it is possible to engage in a discussion about the political origins of underdevelopment across a broad range of disciplinary perspectives.

Contributors

STEPHEN HABER is Peter and Helen Bing Senior Fellow at the Hoover Institution and professor of history and political science at Stanford University. He is also the director of Stanford's Social Science History Institute.

ANNE O. KRUEGER is a senior fellow of the Hoover Institution and Herald L. and Caroline L. Ritch Professor of Humanities and Sciences in the Department of Economics at Stanford University. She is also the director of Stanford's Center for Research on Economic Development and Reform. In June 2001, she was appointed first deputy managing director of the International Monetary Fund.

NOEL MAURER is an assistant professor of economics at the Institutio Tecnológico Autónomo de México.

ARMANDO RAZO is a Ph.D. candidate in political science at Stanford University.

KENNETH L. SOKOLOFF is a professor of economics at the University of California at Los Angeles and a research associate of the National Bureau of Economic Research.

WILLIAM SUMMERHILL is an associate professor of history at the University of California at Los Angeles. During academic year 1999–2000 he was a national fellow at the Hoover Institution.

AARON TORNELL is an associate professor of economics at the University of California at Los Angeles.

Stephen Haber

Introduction:
The Political Economy
of Crony Capitalism

Since the Asian economic collapse of 1997 scholars and policy-makers have grown increasingly interested in the phenomenon of crony capitalism. Indeed, much of the surprisingly rapid meltdown of the East Asian economies is often attributed to widespread cronyism.

Yet although crony capitalism is frequently offered as a description or explanation of the inefficient economic systems of much of the developing world, the phenomenon remains poorly understood. Why do crony economic systems come into being? Why, exactly, are such systems bad for growth? If crony systems are bad for growth, then why do they survive for so long? Finally, under what conditions can crony capitalism be reformed?

This volume does not seek to offer definitive answers to these questions. The state of our knowledge is not yet well enough developed. This volume does, however, advance a set of tentative answers to these questions that we hope will motivate and guide future research.

Although crony systems can be found in a broad range of countries, we focus primarily (although not exclusively) on Latin America. We do so for the following reasons. First, an overlap in our empirical studies brings a degree of coherence to the chapters that would be more difficult to accomplish otherwise. Second, Latin

America provides an ideal natural laboratory to study the causes and consequences of cronyism. Indeed, there is perhaps no region of the world in which crony arrangements have been as fundamental a feature of the economy as in Latin America.

Crony capitalism is usually thought of as a system in which those close to the political authorities who make and enforce policies receive favors that have large economic value. These favors allow politically connected economic agents to earn returns above those that would prevail in an economy in which the factors of production were priced by the market. Frequently, the factor of production that is provided cheaply to cronies is capital. Cheap credit is funneled to the enterprises of cronies through government-controlled banks. This type of entitlement does not, incidentally, require a state-run banking system. Under crony systems, even private bankers can be induced to provide credit to insiders so long as the bankers themselves receive some form of economic entitlement from the government in exchange. Cronies may also be rewarded with the ability to charge higher prices for their output than would prevail in a competitive market. Indeed, one very common form of entitlement is to award a favored economic group with an official or quasi-official monopoly, thus allowing that group to earn monopoly rents. Even if it is not possible to create a monopoly, however, cronies can still be protected from international competition by high levels of trade protection. This allows cronies to earn rents through the ability to charge prices well above those that prevail internationally. In fact, if the trade regime requires that firms obtain licenses to import certain key inputs, governments may use the selective award of these licenses to create monopolies in industries that otherwise would be characterized by more competitive markets.

Why do governments grant such favors and create such entitlements? The answer is that crony capitalism is a solution, albeit a second-best one, to a fundamental problem faced by all governments: Any government strong enough to protect and arbitrate property rights is also strong enough to abrogate them. The ability of the government to arbitrarily predate on asset holders creates a dilemma. Unless the government can find a way to tie its hands, asset holders will not invest. If asset holders do not invest, there will be no economic growth. And if there is no economic growth, the government will be unable to finance its needs because there will be insufficient tax revenue.

How can a government create a credible commitment that it will not use its powers either to tax away all of the rent created by property rights or completely abrogate those rights? Simply promising to do so is not enough. The government can always break the promise at some later point. Indeed, the government may have strong reason to break the promise later because it faces some dire emergency or threat.

The question of how governments tie their hands has motivated a great deal of research by political scientists and has spawned a broad literature on what has come to be known as the *commitment problem*. That research, however, has focused principally on countries such as the United States. These countries solve the commitment problem through the creation of limited governments. Limited governments are understood as those that respect due process and universal individual political and economic rights—and that are bound to respect these rights through sets of self-enforcing institutions. The exact structure of these institutions varies across states. In general, however, they take the form of multiple, overlapping veto points in the decision structure of the government. Individual political actors cannot implement policies without the approval of other actors. The system is set up in such a way that the benefits to any individual actor from staying within the constitutional structure exceed those from going outside it. In the United States, for example, the president is limited by a bicameral legislature, an independent judiciary, state and local governments, and a set of independent federal agencies with professionalized civil service staffs. Thus, the U.S. president cannot arbitrarily renege on an agreement with a private individual because he or she would be blocked by (or subject to sanctions from) other branches and levels of the government. The self-enforcing nature of the institutions that underlie limited governments solves the commitment problem. Precisely because the government cannot act in an arbitrary manner, asset holders will invest.[1]

Most countries do not, however, have limited governments. They must solve the commitment problem in some other way. That is, they must find a way to tie their hands but cannot or will not create the mechanisms of limited government. We would argue that, absent limited government, a common solution to the commitment problem is crony capitalism. Essentially, crony capitalism allows government to guarantee a subset of asset holders that their property rights will be protected. From the individual asset holder's point of view, whether property rights are universal or particular is irrelevant. As long as their assets are protected, these asset holders will continue to invest as if there were universal protection of property rights. Thus, economic growth can occur, even though the government is not limited.

1. See Douglass C. North, *Structure and Change in Economic History* (New York: Norton, 1981), pp. 146–57. Also see Margaret Levi, *Of Rule and Revenue* (Berkeley: University of California Press, 1988); Barry R. Weingast, "The Political Foundations of Limited Government: Parliament and Sovereign Debt in 17th- and 18th-Century England," in John N. Drobak and John V.C. Nye, eds., *The Frontiers of the New Institutional Economics* (San Diego: Academic Press, 1997), pp. 213–46; Douglass C. North and Barry R. Weingast, "Constitutions and Commitment: The Evolution of Institutions Governing Public Choice in Seventeenth-Century England," *Journal of Economic History* 49, no. 4 (December 1989): 803–32; Douglass C. North, *Institutions, Institutional Change, and Economic Performance* (Cambridge, England: Cambridge University Press, 1990); Barry R. Weingast, "The Political Foundations of Democracy and the Rule of Law," *American Political Science Review* 91 (1997): 245–63; Kenneth Shepsle, "Discretion, Institutions, and the Problem of Government Commitment," mimeo, 1991; and Hilton L. Root, "Tying the King's Hands: Credible Commitments and Royal Fiscal Policy during the Old Regime," *Rationality and Society* 1: no. 2 (October 1989): 240–58.

How are such arrangements made credible? What keeps the government from unilaterally changing the rules once the asset holders have invested their wealth in productive assets? More extremely, what keeps the government from confiscating these productive assets?

The answer is that members of the government itself, or at least members of their families, must share in the rents generated by the asset holders. This may take the form of jobs, coinvestments, or even transfers of stock. It is why crony capitalism goes hand in hand with corruption. What matters is that any attempt by the government to change the economic policies that benefit the asset holders will have a negative effect on the wealth and happiness of crucial members of the political elite that support the government. The activities of Suharto's family in Indonesia are a classic example of this phenomenon: the dictator's own family received rents from just about every enterprise in the country, which constrained the dictator from seizing private assets. In short, the intermingling of economic and political elites means that it is extremely difficult to break the implicit contract between government and the privileged asset holders.

Crony capitalism is not, however, as good a solution to the commitment problem as limited government. From the point of view of economic growth and distribution, crony capitalism has three major drawbacks. First, it encourages the misallocation of resources. The whole point of crony capitalism is that the government designates a set of economic policies that provides some privileged group of asset holders with a high-enough rate of return to induce them to invest without the security of limited government. Without these special entitlements, asset holders would not invest. Thus, crony capitalism not only permits rent seeking, it requires rents to be earned and distributed. Once rent seeking becomes a fundamental part of economic life, however, rent seeking above and beyond the minimum needed to induce investment will almost inevitably occur. In fact, asset holders must share some of the rents with crucial members of the political elite (in order to secure the implicit contract between the asset holders and the government). The level of rent seeking must therefore be even higher still. Industries will exist that would not exist otherwise, monopolies and oligopolies will exist in industries that should be characterized by more perfect competition, and opportunities will be denied to entrepreneurs who have the required skills and assets but not the political access or protection required. In short, crony capitalism is economically inefficient.

Second, the fact that crony systems ultimately depend on the personal connections of particular asset holders and government actors means that the commitments of the government are credible only so long as that particular government is in power. This stands in stark contrast to limited government, in which government commitments are made credible by the fundamental institutions of the polity, regardless of the identity of the individuals exercising power. Under a crony system, if the government is replaced, those personal connections vanish and with them the protection of the property rights of even privileged economic groups. For this reason, economic agents under crony systems, including the politically connected, will operate with short time horizons. This causes cronies to demand high rates of return even for projects that have short maturities. It may, in fact, completely discourage long-term investing.

Third, crony capitalism has negative consequences for the distribution of income. In a crony system, some privileged asset holders must be able to earn rents in order to induce them to invest. These rents must come from somewhere: usually everyone else in the society. Imagine, for example, that a group of cronies has obtained from the government a monopoly on some important line of economic activity, such as banking or telecommunications. Its politically created monopoly will allow it to charge prices for services well above what would prevail under conditions of free entry. Essentially, then, there will be a transfer of income from everyone using telecommunications or banking services to the managers and shareholders of those firms.

The economics of crony capitalism are taken up at length in the first chapter of this book, "Why Is Crony Capitalism Bad for Growth?" In this chapter, Anne Krueger examines the efficiency effects of crony systems by drawing parallels between the economic arrangements of cronyism and those of state-owned enterprises. This allows her to solve a crucial problem in the economic analysis of cronyism; by definition, crony arrangements are not transparent and the costs of cronyism are hidden as profits. She argues, however, that state-owned enterprises are almost exactly the same in their effects as cronyism—and for exactly the same reasons. She is therefore able to draw on evidence about the performance of state-owned enterprises to provide her with a window with which to view the performance of crony enterprises. She then extends this analysis to the study of the how cronyism can take place through the trade regime, focusing in particular on the use of import licenses in import-substituting countries and inexpensive domestic credit in export-oriented countries.

If crony systems are bad for growth, then why do they persist for so long? Why and how do crony systems get re-created over time, even in the face of dramatic regime changes? The answer is that every government that comes to power, regardless of its stated ideology, faces exactly the same commitment problem as the government it replaced. Unless it can make the very difficult transition to limited government, it will find itself confronting the same dilemma as the crony system that replaced it; if it does not create entitlements for a select group of asset holders, there will be no investment and economic growth, and if there is no investment and economic growth, the government's ability to tax will be constrained.

The persistence of crony systems is taken up at length by Stephen Haber, Noel Maurer, and Armando Razo in the second chapter of this volume, "Sustaining Economic Performance under Political Instability: Political Integration in Revolutionary Mexico." Drawing on the economics literature on industrial organization, Haber, Maurer, and Razo develop a model of the economics of crony systems. They then use an archetypal case of a crony system, the Porfirio Díaz dictatorship in Mexico (the period 1876–1910), to show how, as a practical matter, governments make credible commitments to protect property rights by providing small groups of asset holders with special entitlements. Finally, they show how this crony system was re-created after Díaz was overthrown and a new government came to power. They argue that even though Mexico fought a violent revolution that brought to power a government with a radically different ideology than that of Díaz, all the postrevolutionary governments engaged in precisely the kinds of cronyism that Díaz had. In fact, many of the cronies before and after the revolution of 1910–1920 were exactly the same people.

Crony capitalism is not solely an economic phenomenon. It is a political creation and has political consequences. Crony systems require that special economic entitlements be granted to some subset of asset holders. These entitlements then allow those asset holders to extract rents from other members of society. Electoral democracy, however, would rapidly erode these entitlements: the losers from rent seeking would presumably mobilize and defend their interests. Under crony capitalism, therefore, the government must be able to make deals in smoke-filled rooms without public review and approval; crony systems are not consistent with high levels of political democracy. Indeed, the more authoritarian the government, the more efficiently the system can work.

The connection between political institutions and crony capitalism is discussed at length in the chapters by Kenneth Sokoloff and William Summerhill. Sokoloff's point of departure is that the rules of political organization have a fundamental impact on the policy choices of governments. He therefore focuses on the conduct of elections under crony systems, paying particular attention to the question of who holds the right to vote. His chapter, "The Evolution of Suffrage Institutions in the New World: A Preliminary Look," compares the experiences of Latin America with those of the United States from the time of independence to the present day. His findings are striking. Where there was extreme economic inequality, the proportion of the population that had the right to vote at the time of political independence was generally low. Moreover, in areas characterized by extreme inequality, the timing of the extension of the right to vote from elites to a broader population generally occurred later. In fact, even though most New World polities were at least nominally democratic by the middle of the nineteenth century, only a few had electoral laws allowing universal male suffrage before the twentieth century. In some extreme cases, such as Brazil, literacy and property restrictions on suffrage were not dropped until recently.

The chapter by William Summerhill, "Party and Faction in the Imperial Brazilian Parliament," pursues the issue of the relationship between political organization and crony systems through a detailed analysis of a single case: nineteenth-century Brazil. Brazil is perhaps an ideal case with which to study the political consequences of a crony economic system—political authority was highly centralized and suffrage was tightly restricted. Summerhill notes, however, that well-developed party systems would have mitigated some of the effects of political centralization; by forcing legislators to act in concert, parties can override narrow constituent interests and thereby curtail pork-barrel politics. His major findings for the Brazilian case can be summarized as follows. Contrary to what scholars have long believed, political parties mattered a great deal in nineteenth-century Brazil. Parties commanded considerable electoral resources that were valued by federal deputies. The Brazilian Chamber of Deputies therefore adopted policies that were less distortionary than would have existed otherwise. The magnitude of this party effect cannot be estimated with precision, but the general result is clear: political parties gave rise to economic policies that mitigated the negative consequences of Brazil's highly centralized political system.

One of the implications of the Sokoloff and Summerhill chapters is that crony systems can be reformed. In the long run, changes in the rules concerning suffrage and the development of strong political parties should erode the discretionary power of the government to grant lucrative (and economically distortionary) entitlements. The chapter by Haber, Maurer, and Razo, however, suggests that such reforms might not be easy to accomplish; any government that comes to power will still confront the commitment problem.

The issue of reformability of crony systems is pursued by Aaron Tornell in the final chapter of this volume, "Economic Crises and Reform in Mexico." Tornell begins his analysis by noting that Mexico carried out a series of fundamental economic reforms during the 1980s and 1990s. These reforms, which deregulated much of the Mexican economy and opened it up to foreign trade and investment, had a negative effect on a politically powerful groups of cronies. Why is it that these power holders, to use Tornell's phrase, did not block the reforms, even though all or most of these reforms resulted in conditions that made the power holders worse off? Tornell argues that reforms occurred in Mexico because the economic crisis generated by cronyism itself produced conflict among the powerful economic groups. Some groups unilaterally relinquished their privileges because they sought to prevent other groups from introducing changes that would harm them even more or because they sought to neutralize the harmful effects of changes already introduced by other groups. Once this process began, it proved difficult to stop.

One of the implications of Tornell's chapter is that fundamental economic reforms to crony systems may only be possible during a period of severe economic crisis. When the economy is doing well, every politically powerful economic group finds that the short-run diversion of resources that would be necessitated by economic reform exceeds the benefits that the group might attain. It is only during an economic crisis, when the opportunity costs of diverting resources fall, and when groups fear reforms induced unilaterally by other groups, that the implicit coalition between the cronies breaks down.

These essays do not, of course, exhaust all the issues related to the political economy of crony capitalism. Indeed, it is our sense that we have only begun to scratch the surface, in terms of both theory and empirical research. Our hope, however, is that the case studies and presented here will provide a point of departure from which further research can be developed.

Why Crony Capitalism Is
Bad for Economic Growth

Until the Asian financial crisis of 1997, economists and policy-makers alike devoted much attention to analyzing the causes of the rapid growth of the East Asian economies. Some viewed their growth as a miracle; others (such as the World Bank) attributed it to high rates of capital accumulation.[1] But regardless of the analyst's conclusions, all wanted to learn the lessons of the East Asian successes in order that other countries might emulate them.

Since the crisis, those same economies are said to have had a large number of failures of economic policy; it is even said that there was no success story. Among the failures, a faulty banking system and cronyism are widely regarded as most fundamental. In this chapter, I examine these conclusions. To do so, I do three things. First, I provide an analysis of cronyism and investigate how and why it might have such negative effects as are now alleged. Second, I consider the role of domestic credit expansion in enabling cronyism and in contributing to the crisis. I then turn to the experience of one East Asian country—South Korea—and provide a possible explanation as to how cronyism and the banking system might have performed so well for so long and then have led to the crisis of late

---

1. See World Bank, *The East Asian Miracle* (New York: Oxford University Press, 1993).

1997. The explanation may apply to other Asian success stories as well—the reason for focusing on Korea is my own comparative advantage in being somewhat more familiar with that economy and economic policies than with the other Asian-crisis countries. Even for Korea, what is suggested is a plausible explanation, rather than a tested and proven hypothesis.

At the outset, however, it is necessary to define cronyism, the subject under discussion. What is normally meant is that some of those close to the political authorities receive favors that have large economic value. Usually, these favors are not outright transfers of wealth (such as forgiving taxes or providing subsidies) but rather take place through provision of economic entitlements. These entitlements can take a variety of forms, but the ones that are most visible in the Asian crisis and the ones under discussion here normally entail ownership of a business or its operation. Ownership may come about when cronies are favored as state-owned enterprises (SOEs) are privatized. More frequently, however, economic entitlements have arisen by enabling the cronies—or, more accurately, the establishments they operate, which I shall call crony-operated establishments (COEs)—to receive privileged access to governmental favors that have economic value. It is a reasonable guess, although it would be hard to devise an empirical test, that the quantitatively most valuable favors received by COEs have been provision of monopoly or quasi-monopoly positions (often through the granting of import licenses only to COEs or the prohibition of imports of import-competing goods) and the extension of domestic credit at highly implicitly subsidized terms. A third form of cronyism—favoritism in awarding government contracts—is no doubt also important and may in some instances have been quantitatively as significant as the first two forms mentioned above.

Cronyism and Its Effects

Until the Asian crisis, it was widely recognized that SOEs were harmful and negatively affected economic growth prospects in most developing countries. In what follows, I shall argue that SOEs are almost exactly the same in their effects as cronyism and for much the same reasons: in both instances, the enterprises owe their existence not to their performance in a competitive market but to the nonmarket criteria by which they were established and are run. There are, of course, differences: the costs of SOEs are probably more transparent as they are normally financed out of the budget, whereas the costs of cronyism are more hidden in that profits are not necessarily publicly recorded and the value of privileged positions (monopolies, protective tariffs against imports of competing goods, favored access to subsidized credit, etc.) can be difficult to gauge; there may be a slight presumption that cronies are on average somewhat more competent as managers and somewhat more motivated to achieve profits and reduce costs. But, as I shall argue below, these are only mild presumptions, and there is undoubtedly a large random component in the performance of SOEs and of COEs.

Since there is much more analysis of SOE records than of COEs, in significant part because of the greater transparency noted above, it is useful to start by reviewing the ways in which SOEs are understood to be harmful to growth. It is then relatively straightforward to consider how COEs are similar to SOEs.

In some countries, governments have established state-owned enterprises in many lines of activity usually reserved to the private sector in developed countries. SOEs have operated tourist hotels, produced textiles, apparel, and footwear, run steel mills, and been in virtually every line of manufacturing, and most business service, activities. It is widely recognized that SOEs have been loss-making in many countries and have become major fiscal drains. In Turkey, for example, SOE deficits had reached 5.8 percent of GDP by 1980, the year in which economic reform began.[2] Governments that invested heavily in SOEs also attempted to control the private sector by means such as requiring investment licenses, capacity licenses,[3] and/or permits for transporting goods, requiring private sector firms to train, provide housing and other goods and services for their workers, and by imposing price controls. These controls naturally resulted in low rates of return on investment for the private sector unless firms held monopoly positions, often sheltered by import restrictions or prohibitions. Then, private rates of return on capital reflected monopoly positions, not economic rates of return. Since much control over firms was exercised by the authorities, it is reasonable to regard these highly regulated and controlled firms as state-owned enterprises.

In the East Asian countries, however, private firms were generally free to seek profits, and the real rate of return to private capital seems to have (at least until the 1990s—see below) reflected an economic return on capital. Cronyism operated through other mechanisms. In some instances, cronyism resulted from the government's favoring large firms precisely because they were perceived to deliver economic growth. Over time, however, these firms, or more accurately their owners, grew sufficiently powerful that they held considerable influence with top government officials. In many instances, the mechanism for favoring those who were, or became, cronies was the issuance of bank credit.

When rapid economic growth began after policy reforms in the East Asian countries, most had highly underdeveloped banking systems and rapid rates of inflation. Ceilings were imposed on the

2. Organization for Economic Cooperation and Development, *OECD Economic Surveys: Turkey* (Washington, D.C.: OECD Publications and Information Center, 1991), p. 60.

3. Ridiculously enough, capacity licenses generally stipulate the maximum amount it is permissible to produce.

interest rates that banks might charge for lending (or pay to depositors), usually below inflation rates. Those who received loans from the banks at these controlled rates thus received implicit subsidies from the government. In these countries, various mechanisms were used by governments for directing credit. But regardless of how it was done, the favored borrowers profited significantly.

I postpone until the final section an interpretation of how cronyism evolved over time and contributed to the East Asian crisis. I first want to consider the mechanisms through which cronyism might work in terms of a simple analytical framework.

Assume that the only factor of production is capital and that growth occurs via the real rate of return on capital and the extent of capital formation (new investment).[4] In this model, given the pool of investible funds, the real rate of return on capital determines the total increment in output:

$$DY = R \; DK = R \; I = RS$$

I start by taking S, or savings, as the increase in the capital stock and hence investment, I, as given.[5] Except when explicitly stated

4. To make the model more realistic, one could add labor as a factor of production. If the population were growing, the real rate of return on capital would be driven by the change in the capital-labor ratio as well as by the degree of imperfection in the allocation of new investment. The complication would add little to the basic analysis presented below, although a declining real rate of return on capital could reflect a rising capital output ratio as well as the sorts of phenomena discussed here. This qualification is important for interpreting the East Asian experience and is addressed somewhat later in the section on cronyism in East Asia.

Also for simplicity, I assume that capital does not depreciate. Amendments to the model to account for depreciation would not change the results substantively, and the existence of depreciation can readily be taken into account in applications, as can be seen in the section on cronyism in East Asia.

5. In reality, there were sizable capital inflows in most of the East Asian economies that augmented domestic savings. When these flows were in forms that went through the banking system and were monetized, they accentuated the problems discussed below. When, instead, they were direct investments (offset by imports of machinery and equipment), their effect would have been just the same as an increase

otherwise, it will be assumed that the total level of investment equals domestic savings and is exogenous. I focus on R, the real rate of return on capital. The aggregate real rate of return is itself a weighted average of the rates of return on individual investments times the share of those investments in total investments:

$$R = \text{sum} \ (RI \times FI),$$

where RI is the real rate of return to capital in economic activity I and FI is the fraction of investment directed toward activity I.

In a perfectly competitive textbook economy, of course, the rate of return on each investment is equal and an efficient allocation of resources—in this case investment—results. Over time, the real rate of return on investment might fall if the capital-labor ratio rose and there were diminishing returns to capital. But diminishing returns to capital are less likely to occur at any significant speed in small open economies, where world demand for their tradable goods is highly elastic,[6] than they would be in a closed economy, where the price of the outputs of labor-intensive goods would start declining as output expanded.

Now consider a two-sector economy in which investments are made. One sector is public: it includes SOEs and highly regulated, privately owned firms (presumably in import-substitution activities).[7] The other is an economically efficient private sector (producing exportables, unprotected import-competing goods, and home goods in competitive activities that respond to appropriate relative

---

in total savings and an equal increase in private-sector investment. For that reason, little is gained by explicitly considering capital flows in the model.

6. For a model demonstrating this high elasticity, see Jaume Ventura, "Growth and Interdependence," *Quarterly Journal of Economics* 107, no. 1 (February 1997): 57–84.

7. In the real world, these activities often include banking services, insurance, and other finance, as foreign firms are often ineligible to participate. In some instances, these activities are run by SOEs.

prices of inputs and outputs (i.e., world prices for outputs and market-determined factor prices that reasonably reflect opportunity cost). Then assume an allocation mechanism for investment between the efficient private sector, with a rate of return of RP across investments, and state-owned enterprises, with a rate of return RS. By construction, RS is less than RP and may be negative. Then the rate of return on total investment will be

$$R = FP \times RP + (1 - FP) \times RS,$$

where R is the economywide rate of return on investment and FP is the fraction of investment going to the public sector.

The growth rate for the economy will be

$$GY = R \times I/K = R \times S/K,$$

where S is the economy's aggregate savings and equals the economy's aggregate investment, I.

Clearly, the rate of growth will be lower than attainable, and it will be lower by more, the greater the fraction of investment allocated to the state-owned enterprises and the larger the differential between the private and the public sector's rate of return. In many developing countries, state-owned enterprises—not even counting highly regulated private firms—accounted for as much as 50 percent of all savings and rates of return were zero or lower, while rates of return on private economic activity were arguably on the order of 10 percent or higher. The economywide rate of return in those cases would have been about 5 percent, whereas the attainable rate would have been 10 percent (had there been little or no diminishing returns to private investment).[8] If the savings rate was 20 percent, lost

---

8. Reality is more complicated in several ways. Important among them is the consideration that some public investment is directed toward infrastructure. That part is almost certainly complementary to private sector investment. For purposes of the model used here, such infrastructure investment can be regarded as part of private investment.

real growth of GDP would be 1 percent per annum on these numbers. In more extreme cases of SOE losses at a rate of 5 percent of capital, a 25 percent savings rate, and a 15 percent rate of return on private investment with half of all investment allocated to SOEs, the growth forgone equals the difference between the 3.75 percent increment of GDP that would occur if all savings were allocated to private investment and the 1.25 percent growth that would actually take place—a 2.5 percentage point reduction in the rate of growth of GDP.[9]

This model can be complicated in a number of ways: The domestic savings rate could be an increasing function of the overall return on investment, in which case the savings rate would increase as the fraction of investment going to the private sector increased.[10] In the extreme case given above, if the domestic savings rate fell from 30 percent when the real rate of return was 15 percent to 20 percent when the real rate of return averaged 5 percent, the resulting drop in the growth rate from capital accumulation would be from an attainable 4.5 percent to 1.0 percent, with half of investment allocated to the SOEs.

One could also make savings a function of disposable income and model the government budgetary process as one in which taxes

9. These illustrative estimates are based on recorded orders of magnitude; if one followed the model, one would first estimate the fraction of private enterprise that was heavily regulated and controlled and combine that investment with that of SOEs and return on capital to attain a more accurate number. It will be seen below that the estimated rates of return in Korea are considerably higher than even these numbers suggest for the private sector during the years of rapid growth.

10. In Korea, the savings rate rose steadily after 1960 as the rate of growth of income and the real return to savers rose. It is possible, of course, that the substitution effect toward more savings could be outweighed by the income effect and that savings might fall. For present purposes, however, that does not seem relevant in light of the East Asian experience and the dramatic increases in savings rates that took place (whether because of high marginal propensities to save out of higher incomes or because of a strong response to high real returns).

were increased to cover SOE losses or the take of cronies, to anticipate an argument below.

One could also model a country in which politicians took as a goal that a specified target percentage of output should originate in public sector enterprises, in which case alpha *s* would be rising over time as the return on private investment threatened to increase the relative size of the private sector; with the declining share of investment in the private sector, the growth rate could drop even further. The state enterprises might experience a declining rate of return on investment over time, as politicians saddled enterprises with excess staff, poor location, and other costs. As the rate of return turned negative, growth would decelerate. If one combined the declining rate of return on investment with the share of output target, the overall rate of growth could decline over time and, if the real rate of return on public sector enterprise investments turned negative, could indeed become negative.[11]

Since population growth rates are positive in developing countries and high in many, labor force growth is also a source of real GDP growth. For countries with rapidly growing populations, however, the difference of 2 or 3 percentage points of real GDP growth per annum can be the difference between rising real per capita incomes and standards of living and falling ones.

An interesting issue—connected with cronyism—arises with regard to the granting of monopoly positions; in many countries, SOEs were established to produce import-competing goods; once the SOE was in production, imports were no longer permitted, and the SOE had a monopoly of that particular good. The economic rate of return to such an activity was negative to the extent that resources

---

11. Losses in SOEs and their continued importance in investment are certainly part of the story of poor economic performance in many countries of sub-Saharan Africa. It is estimated that, in India, the SOEs accounted for about 80 percent of all manufacturing investment and about 25 percent of output. See Pranab Bardhan, *The Political Economy of Development in India* (Oxford: Basil Blackwell, 1984), p. 102.

that could have earned a higher return in other activities were diverted to the SOE; with monopoly rents, however, some SOEs were financially profitable. For purposes of analyzing cronyism, the granting of monopoly positions can be regarded as a form of taxation (of consumers or private producers, depending on whether the SOE produces final consumer goods or intermediate goods) with a commensurate rise in the savings rate to cover the economic losses associated with the enterprise. In the national income accounts, of course, monopoly profits accruing to state-owned enterprises are treated no differently than other profits, and the opportunity costs of resources allocated to high-cost, import-competing industries are not reflected.

Before considering cronyism directly, it is useful to consider one possible variant of the SOE model. That is, suppose that, instead of investing in SOEs at negative real rates of return, the government were to use resources to provide for palaces, airplanes, luxury automobiles, and other luxuries for the ruling group, or elite. Suppose that a fraction of savings, equal to that allocated to SOE investments in the situation outlined above, was diverted to these purposes through taxation or through deficit financing (including possibly even borrowing from abroad).

To analyze the effects on growth, there must be two additional specifications. The first question is whether the palaces, airplanes, and luxury automobiles are maintained at public expense. The second is how these expenditures are recorded in the national accounts. Consider first the case where the airplanes, palaces, and other consumption items are maintained at private expense once diverted to the ownership of the elite and where these expenditures are recorded in the national income accounts as investments. In that circumstance, the rate of return on these expenditures is zero, and the case is precisely the same as that modeled above, with the specification that the return on investment is zero. If, instead, these expenditures are recorded as consumption, the domestic savings rate falls commensurately, but the impact on growth is identical. Of course, if the resources to finance the consumption expenditures (or the SOE investments) are raised in ways that reduce the domestic savings rate, the negative impact on growth is even greater.

If the palaces, airplanes, and other luxury items are maintained at public expense, however, the ensuing maintenance costs are equivalent to losses incurred by SOEs.[12] If maintenance costs are a constant fraction of the stock of these consumption goods, and the stock of such items increases more rapidly than output over time, the overall rate of economic growth will decline unless the capital stock rises at an increasing rate.

With this simple framework we can now address the basic issues that arise with cronyism. Perhaps the basic question is what cronyism is. It might be the exemption from taxes or the direct allocation of consumption goods to a favored individual or group. In that case, the effects of cronyism on resource allocation and growth are no different from the effects of any other tax to finance government consumption or subsidy to some private economic activities. The effects of cronyism would be little different from the effects of such activities as a subsidy to the consumption of fertilizer or food grains.

However, suppose instead that the cronyism consists of extending to some individuals or groups favored status with respect to entry into economic activity. It is this form of cronyism that has been the focus of concern in East Asia. In countries pursuing import-substitution policies, this favoritism was exercised through the granting of import licenses for capital or intermediate-goods imports to these favored groups. Since foreign exchange was overpriced, it was rationed; since imports of most import-competing

12. For simplicity, I ignore the accounting and other questions surrounding depreciation and assume that investment and consumption items are infinitely lived.

goods were highly restricted, there was a monopoly profit conferred with the granting of these licenses. Cronyism could therefore take place through the trade regime and the import licensing that accompanied it. Activities that were privately profitable (because of monopoly positions) were socially unprofitable.

For countries pursuing outer-oriented trade strategies, however, favors could not be conveyed through privileges associated with the import regime. An alternative mechanism was to create a climate in which real rates of return on investment were high, and in which financing was available to favored parties at below-market rates of interest (i.e., through extension of domestic credit to favored activities or individuals and groups).

The Role of Domestic Credit in Cronyism

Since in most developing countries inflation rates were relatively high, ceilings on interest rates had the effect of provision of a sizable subsidy element, especially in the context of high real rates of return on investments. In the absence of well-functioning capital markets, a significant portion of new investment was financed by domestic credit creation. With excess demand, governments could direct domestic credit, and therefore resources, toward favored borrowers.

To provide an indication of the relative size and importance of these uses of domestic credit, table 1.1 gives some data for Korea during its period of high growth in the late 1960s. As can be seen, domestic credit was similar in magnitude to gross domestic capital formation, although domestic credit grew more slowly as profits of private sector companies increased. Lending rates of deposit-money banks were around 14 percent in the late 1960s and fell into the single digits by the early 1970s. By contrast, the curb lending rate (the informal market in which most Korean firms borrowed

TABLE 1.1

*Korean Investment Relative to Domestic Credit, and Interest Rates,
1968 to 1972*

	1968	*1969*	*1970*	*1971*	*1972*
Gross domestic capital formation (billion won)	414	556	627	726	831
Domestic credit	469	751	962	1,240	1,600
Credit to private sector	432	706	919	1,201	1,463
Lending rate of deposit-money banks (%)	13.4	13.9	8.4	7.8	3.7
Curb loan rate (%)	47.9	44.5	40.6	37.8	25.0
Producer price increase (%)	n.a.	6.8	9.6	8.0	14.2
Implicit subsidy on private domestic credit (billion won)	149.0	216.0	295.9	360.3	311.6
GDP	1,630	2,130	2,724	3,379	4,170
Percentage subsidy to private borrowers (% of GDP)	9.1	10.1	10.8	10.7	7.5

SOURCES: Data on gross domestic capital formation, GDP, domestic credit, and producer prices: International Monetary Fund, *International Financial Statistics,* yearbook (Washington, D.C., International Monetary Fund, 1998), Korea country pages. Interest rates: Wontack Hong, "Export Promotion and Employment Growth in South Korea," in Anne O. Krueger, Hal B. Lary, Terry Monson, and Narongchai Akrasanee, eds., *Trade and Employment in Developing Countries,* vol. 1, *Individual Studies* (Chicago: University of Chicago Press, 1981), p. 370 (table 8.14).

beyond the amounts for which they had been eligible through the deposit-money banks) was nearly 50 percent in 1968 and had fallen to only 25 percent by 1972, as the domestic rate of inflation of prices of producer goods rose. If one takes the subsidy element in the provision of domestic credit to the private sector as equal to the differential between the curb rate and the deposit-money bank lending rate, subsidies were equal to between 7.5 and 10.8 percent of GDP over the period 1968 to 1972. Quite clearly, these were quantitatively highly important, especially since a high fraction of

domestic credit was allocated to the export-oriented domestic manufacturing industry, which itself constituted at that time a relatively
small percentage of GDP.

But, for present purposes, the important fact is that domestic
credit was allocated in accordance with government instructions,
and the subsidy element was huge. Insofar as recipients could earn
high real rates of return on investments, they profited enormously.
Wontack Hong has estimated that, in the late 1960s, the real rate of
return on investment in manufacturing was about 37 percent.[13] If
such rates of return were available only to those with access to
domestic credit, the opportunity for profitable cronyism was enormous. The next section of this chapter attempts to explain how
cronyism and its potential for misallocation could coexist with such
a high realized real rate of return.

For present purposes, the point is that cronies can be favored
through the granting of domestic credit when that credit is allocated
at rates significantly below market. If cronies then use the proceeds
to undertake investments that have the highest possible rates of
return, the net effect of credit allocation is simply to transfer income
to them; growth is unaffected. If, however, some (all?) cronies invest
in projects that have lower-than-attainable rates of return (either
because government officials attempt to pick the winners or because cronies are less competent entrepreneurs than those who
would emerge through market processes), the analysis can be undertaken in precisely the same manner as that for the growth effects
of low rate-of-return SOEs: Taking the average rate of return across
crony investments times the fraction of investment undertaken by
cronies and adding that to the rate of return realized among effi-

13. Wontack Hong, "Export Promotion and Employment Growth in South Korea," in Anne O. Krueger, Hal B. Lary, Terry Monson, and Narongchai Akrasanee,
eds., *Trade and Employment in Developing Countries*, vol. 1, *Individual Studies* (Chicago: University of Chicago Press, 1981).

ciently allocated investments times the fraction so allocated will give a growth rate less than that if all investment were channeled through the latter source.

If, however, cronies take some fraction of loan proceeds for their personal consumption expenditures or their Swiss bank accounts, the analysis can again be amended. In particular, to the extent that cronies divert their lines of credit from investment to consumption, the net effect on growth can be treated as equivalent to investments with a zero rate of return or, alternatively, a fraction of investable funds that are diverted to consumption. If investments in SOEs yield a positive real rate of return while cronies simply divert the domestic credit extended to them to their private uses, SOE investments may prove superior to extension of domestic credit to cronies.

A final case needs to be considered. Assume that cronies have invested in loss-making enterprises but that, for whatever reasons, the authorities direct the banks to maintain evergreen accounts for the cronies. Under this arrangement, interest on the outstanding volume of bank credit is treated as paid and new loans to the cronies are extended in the amount of the interest; nonperforming loans do not show up on the books at all. If the banks do not extend any additional credit, cronies cannot invest, as there are no profits and their incremental domestic credit simply serves to maintain their liquidity.

In those circumstances, funds that otherwise might be directed toward new investment are instead allocated to offset the losses of cronies' firms. In the real world, how such evergreen accounts affect economic activity depends on the accounting undertaken. If firms record their losses and treat interest as paid with an offsetting loss to the company and accumulated debt, the negative returns to cronies will constitute a net subtraction from GDP. If, however, firms fail to record their losses and treat the proceeds of loans as financing new investments, saving and investment will be seen to rise as a percentage of GDP, which in turn will overstate true output by the amount of the losses not appropriately recorded.

Cronyism in East Asia

For the sake of concreteness, I focus the discussion on Korea, although many of the attributes of the Korean economy during its rapid development phase were shared by Taiwan, Hong Kong, and Singapore at similar early stages of development. Moreover, rapid growth began only after major policy reforms had been undertaken.

It is often forgotten that, as of 1960, South Korea had the highest density of population in agriculture of any country in the world, with 70 percent of its population in agriculture; its savings rate was close to zero (with about 10 percent of GDP as investment financed by foreign aid); its per capita income was the third lowest in Asia; its rate of inflation in the mid 1950s had been the highest in the world; it had a multiple exchange-rate regime and a highly restrictive import licensing system with an acute foreign exchange shortage. There were SOEs established in many lines of economic activity, with the usual governmental efforts to control private economic activity.

The list of the woes of the South Korean economy at that time would fill several pages, even at this level of generality. But for present purposes, one other statistic is key to my interpretation of what happened: exports in 1960 constituted about 3 percent of GDP (88 percent of them originating in primary activities), while imports were about 13 percent. This must have meant that the economic return to allocating additional resources to exportables was high, while that to additional resources in import substitution was low or negative. This was borne out by a low real rate of growth of GDP: it had averaged less than 5 percent (with a rate of growth of population of almost 3 percent) from the end of the Korean War to 1960, when the real return should have been high with opportunities for postwar reconstruction.

Between 1960 and 1963, economic policy changed radically. The country's leaders recognized that Korea would not be able to grow without earning more foreign exchange and that foreign aid would not provide a growing source of foreign exchange. Economic incentives were almost reversed. The exchange rate was moved to more realistic levels.[14] Quantitative restrictions on imports were greatly reduced in general and were eliminated for exporters' imports of raw materials, intermediate goods, and capital equipment. Tax policy was reformed and government expenditures rationalized so that the government budget deficit was virtually eliminated. Restrictive labor legislation was removed, with a subsequent increase in real wages at an average annual rate of 8 percent per year between 1964 and 1992 (and an immediate drop in the recorded unemployment rate from around 25 percent in 1960 to around 4 pecent by 1964).

Emphasis switched to achieving economic growth through exporting. Although government officials did not discriminate (at least in the 1960s) between activities (in the sense of favoring exports of one good or service over another—all foreign exchange–earning activities were accorded equal treatment), it can almost be said that they held an export theory of value. Exporters were given priority access to credit (which was, as already indicated, highly subsidized); ports, telecommunications, transport, and other infrastructure supportive of producers were expanded and improved. When an exporter had difficulties with any aspect of filling an order, he had almost immediate access to the president.

There are a large number of interesting aspects to the story. But

14. The real won return to exporters per dollar of foreign exchange was about the same between 1960 and 1970. This was achieved both by occasional exchange rate adjustments until 1964 and then a floating exchange rate and by announcing uniform across-the-board export subsidies and other incentives to exporters that accrued to them automatically.

for my purposes, the important points are these. First, as of 1960, there were enormous opportunities for highly profitable investments in exporting activities, given the distortions in the economy that had earlier discouraged them and the incentives that were then provided. Since it was doubtless economical for almost all new investment to be induced into these newly profitable activities, a credit-rationing regime that directed all credit to finance expansion of capacity for these activities was unlikely to result in serious misallocation of new credit. Moreover, in the early years, there were so many profitable opportunities for export activity that it probably made little difference which ones were in fact chosen. And the skill of the entrepreneurs undertaking them was probably also of second-order importance.

Hence, in the early years of the Korean period of rapid growth under an export-led growth strategy, it seems likely that credit could be and was rationed in ways that were not very different than would have occurred under an efficient market outcome. The resulting rate of growth of exports—a 40 percent per year average annual increase in export earnings from the decade starting in 1963—and the increase in the share of tradables, both exports and imports, in GDP from 3 and 13 percent to 30 percent and more by the 1980s attests to that.

A note about the real rate of return to capital in South Korea, both economy-wide and for manufacturing, is in order here. The economy-wide real rate of return on capital was roughly 60 percent in 1970, falling to about 20 percent by 1980, and remaining at that level until around 1990. The rate of return in manufacturing was lower in the 1970s[15] than the economy-wide rate of return, but by

15. This may reflect estimation error, or it may reflect the huge rural-to-urban migration in the 1970s as farmworkers (with low real wages) migrated to cities and were absorbed in activities with much higher real products. High overall growth, especially in the 1970s, may have been attributable both to the reallocation of labor (with significant increases in the real product of labor) as well as to capital formation.

the late 1970s, the two real rates were similar.[16] Moreover, these rates were falling in the 1990s. By that time, there had been some liberalization of the banking system (with higher nominal and real interest rates) but domestic credit still financed a great deal of capital formation.

Now consider the role of domestic credit. Whereas implicit subsidies to producers were large relative to GDP and investment in the 1960s, they were financing investments with high rates of return. Naturally, in a poor country, the extent of equity of the newly exporting firms was quite low and domestic credit financed a high fraction of expansion. But real rates of return were high, and the allocation of domestic credit caused few problems.

Over time, however, the subsidy element in granting domestic credit decreased as the liberalization of the financial system began. Estimates of this are given in table 1.2, on the assumption that an equilibrium real rate of interest in the financial market would have been 10 percent. As can be seen by comparing those figures to the ones in table 1.1, the subsidy element of domestic credit fell drastically on these assumptions. Moreover, domestic credit expansion as a percentage of GDP—while still too large to be sustainable at a virtually fixed nominal exchange rate—also declined.[17]

At the same time, the firms that had been so favored in the 1960s had become large relative to the Korean economy, and own-

16. In the mid 1970s, a heavy and chemical industry (HCI) drive was begun that targeted specific heavy industries for development. This was the only period during Korea's rapid growth where the government actually attempted to pick the winners and identify individual economic activities. The drop in the rate of return to capital in manufacturing in the late 1970s and early 1980s is probably a reflection of the poor results of the HCI drive; by early 1979, it was already being revamped and was recognized as having put great strains on the economy and jeopardized growth.

17. As long as Asian governments maintained fixed nominal exchange rates, expansion of domestic credit was virtually equivalent to increases in the contingent liabilities of governments. As such, one could regard the unsustainable component of domestic credit expansion as equivalent to financing additional investment through a fiscal deficit.

TABLE 1.2

Korean Investment Relative to Domestic Credit, and Interest Rates,
1990 to 1996

	1990	1991	1992	1993	1994	1995	1996
Gross domestic capital formation (trillion won)	179	215	241	267	305	351	390
Domestic credit	102	125	139	157	186	214	254
Credit to private sector	102	122	136	154	185	213	256
Lending rate of deposit-money banks (%)	10.0	10.0	10.0	8.6	8.5	9.0	8.8
Curb loan rate (%)	n.a.	n.a.	n.a.	n.a.	n.a.	n.a.	n.a.
Producer price increase (%)	4.1	4.7	2.1	1.4	2.7	4.7	2.6
Implicit subsidy on private domestic credit (trillion won)	6	6	3	10	36	10	10
GDP	179	216	240	267	305	351	389
Percentage subsidy to private borrowers (% of GDP)	3.3	2.8	1.2	3.7	11.8	2.8	2.6
Increase in domestic credit as a % of GDP	—	10.6	5.8	5.7	10.1	8.0	11.0

SOURCES: Data on gross domestic capital formation, GDP, domestic credit, lending rate, and producer prices: International Monetary Fund, *International Financial Statistics*, Yearbook, 1998, Korea country pages. Implicit subsidy: calculated as per text.

ers of those firms were important sources of financing for political leaders. In addition, their enterprises accounted for a sizable share of GDP and employment; their favored access to credit had enabled them to expand, and credit rationing skewed toward these firms had apparently constituted a significant barrier to entry or to expansion of small firms.

Because of these factors, and probably also for other reasons, cronyism persisted in the form of favoritism toward the large firms. And, whereas it had been apparently justified by the high real returns earned in the 1960s and early 1970s, there was less justification as the Korean economy matured. Whether the real rate of return fell because of an increased capital-labor ratio and diminishing returns to capital, because of the inability of *chaebol* owners to manage firms in ways appropriate to achieving high returns in the 1990s, or because the chaebol owners diverted domestic credit from their enterprises to maintain or increase consumption expenditures and investment figures are overstated (as the increase in nonperforming loans might suggest) are questions that it is not possible to answer.

Moreover, insofar as there were other economic activities deserving of credit and able to earn higher real rates of return than did the favored firms, the economic effects of the directed credit were the same regardless of which explanation is correct; favoring the chaebol in Korea (and cronies with inappropriate investment schemes or high consumption levels in other East Asian countries) resulted in a slowing growth rate. As the apparent[18] real rate of return to capital fell while the real rate of interest paid on banking lending rose, the degree of subsidy clearly dropped as a percentage of GDP (see table 1.2), and, since the chaebol were larger as a fraction of the Korean economy, the percentage of implicit subsidy fell even further.

Conclusions

There are interesting parallels between SOEs and crony capitalism. With SOEs, low real rates of return and losses are generated for a variety of political reasons: the desire of those in power to

18. I use the word *apparent* because, in some instances, domestic credit was granted to individuals who used the proceeds in two ways that were not investment. In some instances, there are newspaper reports of lending to finance consumption expenditures of cronies; to the extent that these expenditures were recorded as investment, it is not that the real rate of return fell, it is that the rate of investment was overstated. In other instances, domestic credit was extended to firms that were probably making economic losses but concealing the fact by overstating new investments. What appears to be a declining real return may in fact be in part an overstatement of investment.

expand employment despite the absence of productive opportunities; the mislocation of enterprises in favored regions regardless of increased costs; the appointment of managers whose competencies lie in the political rather than the economic arena; the inability to close down uneconomic enterprises; and the soft budget constraint.

In the case of crony capitalism, owners of companies receive credit and may expand because their size is a political asset (too big to fail). They may mislocate in the country's capital to be close to those they wish to influence regardless of cost; since the owners receive subsidized credit regardless of the prospective real returns, cronies can persist in business even when their activities are no longer economic; and since they receive subsidized credit, they in effect have soft budget constraints.

There is another similarity as well: in the case of SOEs, their losses are normally covered by transfers out of central government budgets and increase fiscal deficits. In the cases of cronyism, domestic credit expansion is financed by a capital inflow; the capital inflow is attractive to foreigners because of the government's commitment to maintain an exchange rate. As such, the increase in contingent liabilities of the banking system is parallel in crony capitalism to the fiscal deficit in the case of SOEs.

There is no question that the flaws in the financial system (and the overhang of nonperforming loans) must be addressed before rapid sustainable growth can be resumed. Moreover, especially as international capital markets have learned about emerging markets, there seems less and less choice of exchange rate regimes; only floating exchange rates and possibly currency board systems appear viable. In the future, it will be much more difficult for economies to attract capital inflows through fixing the nominal exchange rate and expanding domestic credit.

But nothing about these lessons implies that the economic growth of the 1960s and early 1970s was not spectacular; it was. Opportunities for high real rates of social and private return were unleashed and were seized with consequent rapid growth. That the financial system was underdeveloped and the criteria for lending were flawed undoubtedly led to some misallocation of loanable funds, although bankers can make mistakes, too. But as the huge opportunities for profit that had arisen because of the alignment of incentives with real payoffs were seized, the economy developed and the scope for misallocation of investible funds increased.

As the real rate of return on capital fell for whatever reason, and the implicit subsidy in domestic credit also dropped, the flaws in the financial system and the commitment to cronies or chaebol became increasingly costly, just as SOE losses mount over time. Whether the problem is crony capitalism or SOEs, it seems evident that long-run satisfactory economic performance can be resumed only when means are found to allocate resources to best uses with arm's-length transactions.

Sustaining Economic Performance under Political Instability: Political Integration in Revolutionary Mexico

If crony capitalism is bad for growth, then why do crony capitalist systems come into existence and persist for long periods of time? This chapter advances a theory about the origins of crony capitalist systems in the special case of unstable polities. We argue that crony capitalist systems—what we term vertical political integration—are the only exit from political instability. Moreover, we argue that such vertically integrated systems do not choke all growth. In fact, growth of a type is possible under vertical political integration, and that growth is robust even to conditions of enduring political instability.

A general consensus has emerged in recent years in which limited governments are presumed to provide the political foundations for economic growth. Limited governments are understood as governments that respect due process and universal individual political and economic rights—and that are bound to respect these rights through sets of self-enforcing institutions. The self-enforcing nature of the institutions that underlie limited governments solves a crucial commitment problem: any government strong enough to protect and arbitrate property rights is also strong enough to abrogate them for its own benefit. By creating self-enforcing institutions that constrain the government, private investors will not be restricted by fear of government predation.[1]

In an unstable polity it is impossible, by definition, to create self-enforcing institutions. Political instability should therefore exacerbate the commitment problem. Indeed, factions in an unstable polity will have strong incentives to punish their opponents, reward their allies, levy high taxes on everyone else, and confiscate property in order to finance their political and military activities. There can therefore be no credible commitment by government to not engage in predatory behavior or to change the institutions that govern the economy, and if there are no such credible commitments, there can be no investment and economic growth.

This consensus faces two problems, one empirical and one theoretical. The empirical problem is that we observe large numbers of countries without limited governments that have been able to sustain high rates of economic growth for prolonged periods of time. In fact, economic growth under limited government is a rare com-

1. See Douglass C. North, *Structure and Change in Economic History* (New York: Norton, 1981), pp. 146–57. Also see Margaret Levi, *Of Rule and Revenue* (Berkeley: University of California Press, 1988); Barry R. Weingast, "The Political Foundations of Democracy and the Rule of Law," *American Political Science Review* 91, no. 2 (June 1997): 245–63; Douglass C. North and Barry R. Weingast. "Constitutions and Commitment: The Evolution of Institutions Governing Public Choice in Seventeenth-Century England," *Journal of Economic History* 49, no. 4 (December 1989): 803–32; Douglass C. North, *Institutions, Institutional Change, and Economic Performance* (Cambridge: Cambridge University Press, 1990); and Barry R. Weingast, "The Political Foundations of Limited Government: Parliament and Sovereign Debt in 17th-and 18th-Century England," in John N. Drobak and John V.C. Nye, eds., *The Frontiers of the New Institutional Economics* (San Diego: Academic Press, 1997). On the problem of commitment, see Gary J. Miller, *Managerial Dilemmas: The Political Economy of Hierarchy* (Cambridge, New York, and Melbourne: Cambridge University Press, 1992); Robert Barro and David Gordon, "Rules, Discretion and Reputation in a Model of Monetary Policy," *Journal of Monetary Economics* 12 (1983): 101–21; Kenneth Shepsle, "Discretion, Institutions, and the Problem of Government Commitment," mimeo, 1991; and Hilton L. Root, "Tying the King's Hands: Credible Commitments and Royal Fiscal Policy during the Old Regime," *Rationality and Society*.

bination found in only a small set of nations. Economic growth, however, can be found within a broad range of political systems.

The theoretical problem is the absence of an adequate framework to analyze the phenomenon of political instability. Much of the existing literature defines political instability the same way Justice Potter Stewart defined obscenity: we know it when we see it. Unfortunately, without an adequate definition of instability we cannot then develop a theory of how private individuals can mitigate the effects of instability or how governments can make credible commitments under unstable conditions. That is, without a theoretical framework, we cannot understand how it would be possible to achieve economic growth without limited government.

In fact, the current literature gives few possible exits from political instability. In order to gain enough power to establish political dominance, a government or faction under instability needs economic resources. Unfortunately, if a government under these conditions limits its predation, it will soon fall to a faction with less scruples. Although this may be a good description of much of human history, recent centuries suggest that there must exist some sort of "exit strategy" from pernicious instability other than the establishment of limited parliamentary regimes.[2]

The solution we explore to the problem of credible commitment under conditions of political instability is similar to that used by firms in situations where bilateral, self-enforcing contracts are impossible and there is no recourse to third-party enforcement at a reasonable price: vertical integration.[3] In other words, government

---

2. In fact, limited governments seem remarkably poor at exporting their institutions. Witness the experience of the Philippines after four decades of American colonial rule. Other than cases of complete absorption (such as Hawaii or Puerto Rico), the only successful case of the foreign imposition of clear-cut limited government that we can think of is the creation of the Federal Republic of Germany after the Second World War.

3. See Benjamin Klein, Robert G. Crawford, and Almen Alchian, "Vertical

and economic groups (or competing factions) integrate, either backward by allowing economic actors to write and enforce the rules governing their own activities in return for support for the government or forward by encouraging politicians to directly engage in productive and lucrative economic activity.[4] By integrating, the government can promise to respect property rights (at least those of the integrators) and private actors can credibly pledge their support for the government. Economic activity, then, can be sustained under conditions of political instability if governments can integrate sufficiently to give favored actors confidence that their interests will be protected. In fact, certain economic groups may come to perceive that any faction that comes to power will have to backward-integrate into this group. Partial integration can be enough to sustain economic activity if it encourages unintegrated or partially integrated private actors to believe that they are in a repeated game with other, more-integrated actors and the government.

Vertical political integration, as we will explore below, is clearly a second-best solution compared to limited government. However, absent particular historical circumstances, it is often the only feasible way of sustaining economic activity, especially if instability is considered the starting point. When there is political instability, an immediate jump to limited government and its accoutrements—universal political rights, due process of law—is difficult to impossible. As we will show, under instability the governance structures necessary to solve the commitment problem do not lead to limited government, but they can and do support economic growth. In fact, in the case we explore here, vertical political integration served as

---

Integration, Appropriable Rents, and the Competitive Contracting Process," *Journal of Law and Economics* 21, no. 2 (October 1978): 297–326.

4. Mexico under the PRI and prerevolutionary France are good examples of the first sort of integration, while Eastern Europe under communism is perhaps the most extreme example of the second.

the political foundation of growth both before and after the Mexican Revolution. Not only did both pre- and postrevolutionary governments vertically integrate into elite economic groups: they often integrated into precisely the same economic groups as their predecessors.

We organize this chapter as follows: The first section presents our theory about the feasibility of credible commitments under political instability through vertical political integration. The second section presents a brief history of the Porfiriato and the revolution years. The third section discusses the vertical political integration that took place in postrevolutionary Mexico. We also present some quantitative evidence from the Mexican manufacturing sector to show how vertical political integration was capable of sustaining economic development in the midst of an extreme case of political instability. The fourth section concludes.

Theory

Our theory draws from both the New Economics of Organization and the New Institutionalism. We build on and go beyond both of these bodies of literature in order to create a theory of how it is possible to create credible commitments and encourage investment and growth, even in the midst of widespread political instability.

Political Stability

Before we define political instability, it is appropriate to define a stable political system. Further discussions of instability can then be compared against the benchmark of what we mean by political stability.

A political system is a set of institutions that serve to mediate and organize political interests. More specifically, a political system is the primary source of formal, legally sanctioned, regulations and institutional change in a society. One major purpose of political systems is to decrease uncertainty about two types of political change. The first involves changes in governments.[5] These changes are related to the group of institutions that define the mechanism through which governments are replaced. Institutions that define government selection mechanisms (such as election laws) have an important role in the formation of expectations about who will come to power and what type of institutional changes will be expected. The second type of political change involves fundamental changes in the underlying structure of the political system. This includes changes to the internal rules governing the evolution of the political system as well as changes to the more general mechanisms available for political interaction.[6]

The political system serves as a mechanism to mediate conflicting social demands and produces as output specific rules or policies to govern different types of social interactions, including and extending beyond the political arena. In the case of politics, it provides a division of labor between the public and private sector and delineates the basic rules of political organization that govern a society. In the case of the economy, the political system defines property rights and provides institutions that guide and restrict economic behavior. One notable feature of a political system is that, after the system is first put to work, all subsequent institutional changes are endogenous to the system.

5. Our distinction between a political system and government is similar to the conventional distinction between regimes and governments. However, we prefer the term *political system* because it reflects the ongoing interaction of its elements as opposed to the static definition of regime as a form of government.

6. Our framework is not exclusive of rules that regulate a government after its selection (e.g., constitutional restraints on the executive branch). We include these, if they exist, under the second group of rules where the constituents may agree to be governed by a government if the latter conforms to an agreed-upon set of rules (i.e., a constitutional provision that limits its authority). That is, the government—if we assume it has its own objectives—can be one of the agents whose actions are being mediated through the political system. In short, the political system provides rules for the interaction (and permissible behavior) of government and society.

At any point in time, a political system is stable, or self-preserving, if (1) there is common knowledge about the selection mechanism to replace governments and the rules that manage political action and (2) the institutional arrangements that specify this political system are self-enforcing. The first condition has to do with people's beliefs and expectations. It places at the core of our analysis the social relevance of a political system: the extent to which people, in the decisions that they take, internalize the rules that the political system prescribes.[7] The second condition deals with people's actual behavior. That is, a political system is stable when members of society do not deviate from the existing political equilibrium. The stability of the system derives from the common agreement to allow the current political system to mediate conflicting goals in both present and future periods. This common agreement at any point in time is a political equilibrium.

Political Instability

Political instability arises when political stability becomes unsustainable. One cause for instability is the absence of common knowledge about the political system, a situation that we denote as weak instability. Weak instability introduces uncertainty about the future of the current political system because different agents face different institutional environments. In other words, multiple political systems are competing for the governance of society. For example, when a faction succeeds in setting up a "state within a state," as did the Irish Republican Army, for example, or Colombian paramilitaries, it makes rules governing political and social (and often

---

7. It should be noted, however, that most of the work on instability has centered on voting processes occurring at a less aggregated level such as particular elections or decision processes, rather than on the complete set of rules providing the governance structure of a society. See, for example, Peter C. Ordeshook and Kenneth A. Shepsle, eds., *Political Equilibrium* (Boston: Kluwer Nijhoff Publishing, 1982).

economic) life in contradiction of the decisions of government produced by the existing political system.[8]

We have a case of strong instability, however, when the system loses its self-enforcement quality because some political shocks, which would otherwise be internalized or dissipated, become credible threats to the continuity of the political system, making the social contract no longer binding. These threats lead to a situation in which institutional change ceases to be endogenous and is instead subject to the outcome of political competition, often through military means, among factions aspiring to be in government. We further denote instances of strong instability as ex ante revolutions because they are potentially capable of removing the current system and thereby bringing about a discontinuity in the evolution of the political system.[9] Stability is restored upon determination of a new political equilibrium, which may, of course, be its original unpertur-

8. Occasional vigilantism, therefore, is a sign of very weak instability.

9. Notice that our definitions of revolution focus on procedures, which is consistent with our analysis of institutions as rules that constrain social behavior. Thus, exogenous institutional change is revolutionary only because it is not mediated through the existing system. This is a definition that can be used more systematically than one which focuses on the extent and direction of change, in which there is substantial disagreement about the threshold levels beyond which changes can be classified as revolutionary. Most important, our definition links revolutions and instability in a consistent and systematic way. In contrast, other definitions of revolutions as drastic institutional changes preclude the joint study of stability issues simply because any stable political system is capable in principle of producing such changes. This definition is also a bit different from that advanced in Douglass C. North, "Toward a Theory of Institutional Change," in William A. Barnett, Melvin J. Hinich, and Norman J. Schofield, eds., *Political Economy: Institutions, Competition, and Representation* (Cambridge: Cambridge University Press, 1993). There, North characterizes revolutionary change as a situation where "the formal rules may change overnight." As such, it is related to uncertainty in a similar way to ours. However, he adds a critical condition: that the underlying informal institutions concurrently remain unchanged. This produces an internal tension in the overall institutional structure that forces subsequent conflict to be finally resolved in a less revolutionary change. This second part relies more heavily on empirical determination of the extent of formal institutional changes.

bed state. We have a case of ex post revolution, however, when the restored unique system involves substantial institutional changes with respect to the old equilibrium.

Political Instability and the Economy

The four channels through which instability affects economic performance[10] stem directly from the inability of government to protect economic activity. First, instability will make local property rights insecure because it produces a vacuum in the exercise of public laws. This discourages long-term investment in physical capital and economic exchange. Second, without a single political system it is difficult to predict the identity of future governments and the dynamics of future institutional change. This will prompt investors to move their resources to safer and more predictable institutional environments. Third, political instability will increase the probability that individuals will engage in opportunistic rent seeking, thus diverting resources to unproductive purposes.[11] This is particularly true of governments. To the extent that time horizons are shortened, meaning that factions which come to power believe that they will remain in office only temporarily, governments will engage in

---

10. The first two channels can be thought of as direct effects since they stem directly from the existence of instability. The second two are indirect effects since they may occur under other circumstances as well.

11. Gordon Tullock, "The Welfare Costs of Tariffs, Monopolies, and Theft," *Western Economic Journal* 5 (June 1967): 224–32; Anne O. Krueger, "The Political Economy of the Rent-Seeking Society," *American Economic Review* 64 (June 1974): 291–303. Anne O. Krueger, "Virtuous and Vicious Circles in Economic Development," *American Economic Review* 83, no. 2 (May 1993): 351–355; Richard A. Posner, "The Social Costs of Monopoly and Regulation," *Journal of Political Economy* 83 (August 1975): 807–27; Andrei Shleifer and Robert W. Vishny, "Corruption," *Quarterly Journal of Economics* 108 (August 1993): 599–617; Kevin M. Murphy, Andrei Shleifer, and Robert W. Vishny, "Why Is Rent-Seeking So Costly to Growth?" *American Economic Review* 83, no. 2 (May 1993): 409–14; and Paolo Mauro, "Corruption and Growth," *Quarterly Journal of Economics* 10, no. 3 (August 1995): 681–712.

more predatory behavior and rent seeking than they would otherwise. Finally, when political struggles involve the use of force, property will be destroyed. This will discourage investment since prices will have to take this threat into account.[12] Additionally, when violence (organized or unorganized) is widespread, markets will be interdicted, further discouraging economic exchange and therefore production and investment.

Political Instability, Credible Commitments, and Vertical Political Integration

Under instability, factions that come to power cannot make credible commitments to respect property rights. The reason is simple. If a government creates institutions that tie its hands and prevent predation, it will be overthrown by a less scrupulous faction. Similarly, private actors cannot make credible commitments to support particular political factions: they will always have incentives to seek out better deals elsewhere. This means that political contenders under instability must engage in predation in order to remain in the game. Yet, if a faction allows rent seeking in order to reward its supporters, it faces the problem of credibly committing to distribute those rents. Why not, after gaining power, keep all the rents to itself (e.g., engage in predation)?

Instability then places governments (or factions aspiring to become governments) in the same position as a firm trying to contract with agents in a situation where there is no third-party enforcement and both sides have incentives to renege after the contract is signed. Klein, Crawford, and Alchian have argued that under certain conditions firms involved in specialized relationships will have an incentive to integrate rather than abide by a contract. When the costs of contracting are too high, due to potential opportunistic behavior

12. Gregory Clark, "The Political Foundations of Modern Economic Growth: England, 1540–1800," *Journal of Interdisciplinary History* 26 (spring 1996), 565.

to appropriate quasi rents, the inability to enforce contracts or monitor and verify the actions of contracting parties makes it more economical to integrate into one single firm.[13] Political instability creates the same incentives regarding the "specialized relationships" between political factions and economic groups. Just like a firm worried about holdup from suppliers, or suppliers worried about a potential monopsony, the parties' incentives are to integrate vertically.

Vertical political integration involves the creation of a set of governance structures that allow certain economic groups to determine the policies that directly affect them. That is, they allow some economic agents to dictate the institutions that govern their economic activities. We denote this as *backward integration*. There may also be *forward integration*, in which members of the government turn their interest to business enterprise. This creates a commitment mechanism that constrains the government from reneging on current institutional arrangements. By allowing the private sector to have an active (or decisive) role in shaping the institutional framework that governs its behavior, and by linking the fate of the government to the success of the private sector (through forward integration), the government can create a limited commitment to a reduced set of economic agents that it will not predate on their property rights. Thus, economic activity is not necessarily affected by political instability.

Although vertical political integration may create desirable credible commitments, it also has two negative effects. The first concerns the benefits from integration between an economic group and a political group. Economic groups that choose to integrate under instability face a first-mover problem: the first groups to in-

---

13. Benjamin Klein, Robert G. Crawford, and Almen Alchian, "Vertical Integration, Appropriable Rents, and the Competitive Contracting Process," *Journal of Law and Economics* 21, no. 2 (October 1978): 297–326.

tegrate assume the risk that the government will fall, or the faction they are integrating with will fail to take power, leaving them at the mercy of enemies who will need to punish them in order to maintain their own credibility. The rewards from integrating and restoring order, however, are not excludable, unless the integrating economic interests earn some form of economic rent. Therefore, a successful integration strategy not only enables rent seeking, it requires rents to be earned and distributed. This means that in the long run integration is a second-best strategy compared to limited government. The second negative aspect of vertical integration is the potential agency problem that arises when agents (policymakers) abuse the powers delegated to them. Political integration can lessen the principal-agent problem, but it does not eliminate it. As with integration within a firm, it replaces contracting with direct policing of "managerial" activities. In the context of a political system, this implies a relatively high level of authoritarianism.

There is, however, an asymmetry in the incentives for integration and disintegration. Previously disintegrated parties can easily integrate, but once they have integrated, disintegration is difficult. Say, for example, that a government decides to renege on an agreement with its creditors, who have been integrated into the governance structure. It is not clear that they will be able to do so within the institutional framework governing their internal decisions: the bankers are now part of the government, and the government would have to go outside its own decision-making structures in order to renege. In addition, political actors within the government (either the bankers or politicians who have acquired banking interests) will have a strong interest in maintaining the health and profitability of the banking system. Finally, the government will cut itself off from future sources of credit, since (as a fundamental part of any integration strategy) all lending and borrowing must be channeled through the integrated creditors.

It should be noted that there is nothing inevitable about the process of integration between political and economic interests. In a result paralleling the theory of the firm, governance structures are constantly being renegotiated (i.e., these are short-term incomplete contracts) due to unforeseen contingencies. Under political instability, the logic of the situation takes actors to the solution of vertical integration, but the exact workings of the new governance structure are not worked out in detail prior to its enactment. Integration is therefore an iterative process of contracting and recontracting.

Historical Background

What do systems like this actually look like as a practical matter? How do such systems come into being, and how do they reconstruct themselves even during periods of political instability? In this section we discuss Mexico's prerevolutionary political and economic history as background to examine revolutionary Mexico as a canonical case of political instability.

Politics before the Revolution: The Porfiriato Years

Until it erupted in revolution in 1910, Mexican politics had been stable for a thirty-five-year period under the dictatorship of Porfirio Díaz. Díaz had initially faced severe financial and political constraints due to the conditions of political disorder and economic stagnation when he came to power in 1876.[14] Díaz, like his predecessors, had a limited set of instruments to cope with both problems simultaneously. The government could try either to preserve its stay in power and restore stability or to provide a favorable environment for economic activity. If it concentrated on the problem of disorder, it would need to borrow heavily from the private sector, given the

---

14. See Noel Maurer, "Finance and Oligarchy: Banks, Politics, and Economic Growth in Mexico, 1876–1928," Ph.D. diss., Stanford University,1997, for a detailed account of the political economy of the Porfiriato.

lack of an administrative structure that could effectively tax the country's slim economic base. With a long history of predatory governments, the private sector was not willing to lend sufficient funds to the government, leaving governments with the two options: predation (forced loans, arbitrary exactions, and confiscations of property) or collapse. If, instead, the government wanted to promote economic activity by making commitments to respect property rights, then it would have no resources to fight its political opponents and restore political stability.

Díaz's solution to this dilemma was to allow private economic interests to make public policy. This allowed a strong government—a dictatorship, to be exact—to credibly commit to protecting property rights. In essence, the government delegated its policymaking functions to a small group of economic elites. In theory, this should have created an agency problem between the government (the principal) and its delegated policymakers (the agents). This problem was avoided, however, by making the agents the residual claimants on the success of the state. Now the state depended on the economic well-being of the agents, and the agents depended upon the stability of the state.

The integration strategy required huge direct and indirect economic resources. By *direct resources*, we mean the needs of the federal government to pay the army and other federal officials, finance the judiciary, carry out basic government functions, and subsidize the construction of a national railroad network. By indirect resources, we mean the need to create an economy that would generate sufficient rents for the interests with which the government integrated to justify the risks of integration. The first groups to throw their support behind Díaz undertook substantial risks: should his strategy fail, they would be out in the cold, without the direct resources they had lent or given the government and with a substantial stock of political ill-will from his opponents. Only the promise of substantial rents could justify these risks.[15]

The first and most pressing need was for direct resources. Foreign borrowing was out of the question: Mexico had a long and dolorous record of reneging on its international obligations. Therefore, like many governments faced with similar dilemmas, the Díaz government created a bank. In effect, Díaz struck an agreement with a group of domestic and foreign financiers: you lend my government the funds we need to establish a viable government, and I will grant you political protection and a number of extremely lucrative privileges. The agreement "domesticated" the foreign component of these financiers and integrated them into the political structure. In the process, however, Díaz could not simply run roughshod over the interests of the existing banks but had to make major concessions that, while strengthening his short-term political power, effectively limited the federal government's ability to control the financial system in the future.

Essentially, the deal struck between Díaz and the bankers was as follows: The federal government would tightly regulate entry into the banking industry. In return, the nation's largest bank, which received special concessions from the government, would provide the government with a credit line and would act as its financial agent. The result was that two banks carved up virtually all of the Mexico City business and were the only two institutions allowed to branch beyond their state borders. Monopolies were also established at the state level. The federal government committed not to alter this arrangement through forward integration: the secretary of

15. In this sense, the decision of economic elites to support a political faction attempting a strategy of backward integration in the context of political instability is similar to the decision of an innovator to invent a new technique. The first mover undertakes all the risks, but political stability is a public good, which would also be enjoyed by competitors.

the treasury who wrote the laws was also an important shareholder of one of the big Mexico City banks. Much the same situation prevailed at the state level; state governors decided which group of entrepreneurs would receive a federal bank charter (states were not legally able to grant charters) and almost invariably sat on the board of directors of the bank. In return, the largest Mexico City bank (the Banco Nacional de México) agreed to provide the federal government with a credit line and would serve as the government's financial agent.

Similar arrangements took place in manufacturing. Lack of international competitiveness made it necessary for industry to seek trade protection. Díaz provided many of Mexico's new and rapidly growing industries with tariff rates that were extraordinarily high: 76 percent for bottled beer, 72 percent for common cloth, 88 percent for fine cloth, 198 percent for printing paper, 225 percent for candles, and 234 percent for soap, to cite a few examples. In addition, the government created a "cascading" tariff structure: duties on final manufactured goods were high, whereas duties on the inputs to produce those final goods were low or zero.[16] Mexican manufacturing received such high levels of protection because the owners of the major firms were important constituents of the state. They subscribed to the government's bonds; they sat on the boards of the nation's most important financial institutions; and they represented the government in international financial markets when it borrowed money abroad.[17]

16. Calculating the exact level of effective protection requires that researchers have detailed information about the ratio of imported to domestically produced inputs, as well as on the input-output ratio, for each industry. Researchers to date have only been able to demonstrate that over time the ratio of input tariffs fell relative to the tariff on finished manufactures. See Edward Beatty, "The Political Basis of Industrialization in Mexico before 1911," Ph.D diss., Stanford University, 1996, chap. 3.

17. See Stephen H. Haber, *Industry and Underdevelopment: The Industrialization of Mexico, 1890–1940* (Stanford: Stanford University Press, 1989), p. 69. Mexico's

These links between government and special interests operated at both the state and federal levels. In Puebla, the Porfirista governor, Mucio P. Martínez, set up a business that ran several large agricultural estates in partnership with Puebla's powerful group of textile magnates. In return, Martínez often appointed members of this group to his cabinet or the mayoralty of Puebla City.[18] In Nuevo León, the carpetbagging Bernardo Reyes relied on the state's local elite—whom he had displaced with federal support—to serve as mayors, county presidents, state deputies, and federal representatives.[19] In Chihuahua, the Terrazas-Creel clan ran the state as practically a family business enterprise. Luis Terrazas served as governor from 1860 to 1873, 1879 to 1884, and 1903 to 1904, and his son-in-law Enrique Creel followed in the governorship from 1904 to 1910. Their holdings ran across banking, ranching, agriculture, manufacturing, food processing, mining and smelting, dry goods retailing,

---

most important domestic bankers operated on an international scale and had important connections to major foreign banks. See Hilda Sanchez Martínez , "El sistema financiero y monetario mexicano bajo una perspectiva histórica: El Porfiriato," in José Manuel Quijano, ed., *La Banca, Pasado y Presente* (Mexico City: CIDE, 1983), pp. 60–77. Also see *La Semana Mercantil,* June 17, 1901, p. 329; June 30, 1906, p. 367; June 6, 1910, p. 301. For example, Hugo Scherer Jr. (a major industrialist and banker) was a member of the board of the Banco Internacional Hipotecario, which served as a conduit for the movement of capital from New York to Mexico. His international financial connections made him among the most influential bankers in private and government circles. In 1908, for instance, he was asked to handle the sale of 50 million pesos (25 million dollars) worth of bonds in New York to finance the semigovernment-owned Caja de Prestamos para Obras de Irrigación y Fomento de la Agricultura. In addition, Scherer, along with his father, Antonio Basagoiti, and Adolfo Prieto (important textile and steel magnates) sat on the Comisión de Cambios y Monedas.

18. Leticia Gamboa Ojeda, *Empresas y empresarios textiles de Puebla : analisis de dos casos* (Puebla, Pue., Mexico: Seminario de Historia Contemporanea, Centro de Investigaciones Historicas del Movimiento Obrero, Instituto de Ciencias de la UAP, 1986), pp. 192–94.

19. Mario Cerutti, *Burguesia, capitales e industria en el norte de Mexico: Monterrey y su ambito regional (1850–1910)* (Mexico: Alianza Editorial and Facultad de Filosofia y Letras de la Universidad Autonoma de Nuevo Leon, 1992), pp. 360–62.

railroads, and public utilities. By 1910 they were the single largest employer in the state. They also controlled 70 percent of the flour market and 50 percent of meatpacking operations.[20]

Integration may have been a second-best solution in the long run, both politically and economically, but for Porfirian Mexico the long run ran over half a human lifetime. Díaz's institutional reforms produced a long period of rapid economic growth. Foreign investors poured nearly 2 billion dollars into Mexico during the Porfiriato, investing in railroads, ports, urban tramways, export agriculture, ranching, mining, smelting, and petroleum. On the heels of investment by foreigners came a wave of investment by local entrepreneurs in enterprises such as banking, manufacturing, agriculture of all types, some railroad construction, and urban real estate. In 1876 Mexico had only five banks, a minuscule manufacturing sector, and a railroad system that consisted of 400 miles of track, of which 71 used mules rather than steam engines to pull the trains. By 1910, Mexico had a sizable, if concentrated, banking system, a relatively modern manufacturing industry producing a broad range of consumer and intermediate goods, and a railroad system of 17,000 miles that united all the major cities. Mexico had also become one of the world's leading exporters of petroleum, as well as a major producer of various precious and industrial metals. Between 1893 and 1907, Mexico's long-moribund economy achieved real per capita GDP growth of 3.7 percent a year, almost twice as high as in the contemporary United States. Per capita growth over the entire period exceeded 2.7 percent per year.[21]

20. Mark Wasserman, *Capitalists, Caciques, and Revolution: Elite and Foreign Enterprise in Chihuahua, Mexico, 1854–1911* (Chapel Hill: University of North Carolina Press, 1984), chap. 3.

21. Clark W. Reynolds, *The Mexican Economy: Twentieth-Century Structure and Growth* (New Haven: Yale University Press, 1970), p. 21.

Revolution and Political Instability

Space constraints prevent us from providing a detailed exposition of the Mexican revolution and the ensuing period of political instability. Suffice to say that a limited political revolution led by reformist elites was quickly transformed into an ex post revolution. Díaz was overthrown in 1911 and fled to exile in Paris. His reformist successor, Franciso Madero, was overthrown by Díaz's generals within fifteen months of taking office. They, in turn, were driven from Mexico City by a coalition of reformist elites, peasants who clamored for the return of lands that had been confiscated during the Porfiriato, and an increasingly militant working class. That coalition broke apart as soon as it achieved victory in 1914, ushering in three years of civil war. The political victor of that civil war, Venustiano Carranza, was assassinated by his own generals in 1920. His successor, Alvaro Obregón, faced a military uprising led by his own secretary of the treasury in 1923. Obregón was himself assassinated in 1928, the day after he won a second term in office in a rigged election. The army erupted in rebellion on two other occasions in the 1920s, both times over the issue of the presidential succession. When the army was not plotting against the government, it was busy putting down armed insurgencies, the most serious of which was the Cristero Rebellion, a three-year long civil war in which lay members of the church tried to overthrow the government over the issue of the anticlerical measures in the constitution of 1917.

At the same time that all this was happening, the peasants and workers who had been mobilized during the revolution had become politically organized and had in fact pushed through a series of far-reaching reforms at the 1917 constitutional convention. In two areas in particular, Carranza's conservative proposals became transformed into far-reaching, and extremely radical, articles of law: labor relations and property rights. The result was Articles 123 and

27. Article 123 set a maximum workday of eight hours (seven for night work), set limits on the work of women and children, established a six-day workweek, and placed restrictions on the right of employers to fire workers. It also endorsed the principles of a minimum wage, equal pay for equal work, profit sharing, and the indemnification of accidents. Perhaps most fundamentally, it gave workers the right to organize and strike. Finally, it outlined a system of municipal and state-level labor boards (the Juntas de Conciliación y Arbitraje) that would resolve disputes, as well as determine the minimum wage and the appropriate level of profit sharing for each state. In short, the government assumed broad new powers that reduced the rights of employers.[22]

Much to the unhappiness of Mexican employers, Article 123 left the process of creating enabling legislation up to the states. This allowed governors to carry out reforms that went far beyond what Carranza or his successors had in mind. Indeed, for state governors the incentives for doing so were obvious: a politically mobilized working class could provide a governor with the support he might need to challenge attempts by the federal government to curtail his considerable political autonomy.

The constitution of 1917 also redefined property rights. In the decades before the revolution, Porfirio Díaz had carried out a series of policies designed to create secure and clearly defined private property rights in land, intellectual property, and the subsoil. Article 27 of the constitution of 1917 reversed these laws. The residual

---

22. Jeffrey Bortz, "'Without Any More Law Than Their Own Caprice': Cotton Textile Workers and the Challenge to Factory Authority during the Mexican Revolution," *International Review of Social History* 42 (1997): 256–57; Michael M. Hall and Herbert A. Spalding, "The Urban Class and Early Latin American Labour Movements, 1880–1930," in Leslie Bethell, ed., *The Cambridge History of Latin America. Volume 4, 1870–1930* (Cambridge, England: Cambridge University Press, 1986), p. 352; and Joseph E. Sterrett and Joseph S. Davis, *The Fiscal and Economic Condition of Mexico; Report Submitted to the International Committee of Bankers on Mexico* (New York: N.p., 1928), pp. 91–92.

claimant on all property rights became the government. The private ownership of property was no longer considered a right but a privilege, which could be terminated by the government in the public interest. Moreover, subsoil rights, which under Díaz were allocated to the owner of the soil, were specified by the constitution as part of the national patrimony, to be administered by the government. The obvious targets of these reforms were Mexico's agrarian elite and the foreign companies that dominated petroleum and mineral extraction, but their implications were not lost on the holders of other assets, who feared that the government would move to expropriate their property as well. Indeed, they had much to fear: the banking system had undergone a de facto nationalization during the revolution (the Carranza government engaged in direct predation in order to finance its military campaigns against its more radical opponents). In addition, the Carranza government had first reduced the property rights of manufacturers by lowering tariffs in 1917 and then threatened to confiscate factories if the owners closed them to protest the tariff reductions.

Complicating matters even further were powerful state governors who had gained a great deal of political autonomy from Mexico City during the years of revolution. Four governors in particular (Adalberto Tejeda in Veracruz, José María Sánchez in Puebla, Francisco Múgica in Michoacán, and Felipe Carrillo Puerto in Yucatán, known in the conservative press as the "Four Horsemen of the Apocalypse") had cultivated local working-class and peasant constituencies by promulgating their own labor laws and by carrying out de facto agrarian reforms, completely ignoring presidential requests for restraint. This allowed them a high degree of independence from the president. Given their popular support, no president could remove these governors. The best he could do was to deploy conservative generals as local army zone commanders, who often worked with conservative elements in the state to frustrate the populist reforms of the governors and to lean on the federal judiciary (which was not independent) to legally suspend many of the governors' state-level reforms. To cite one example, Governor Adalberto Tejeda of Veracruz created a profit-sharing law in 1921 that required owners to share up to 50 percent of their profits with their workers. Factory owners in Veracruz filed writs of *amparo* (suits seeking a court injunction) against the law. These were openly supported by President Obregón, who used his influence to obtain a favorable ruling from a federal judge.[23]

Thus, it was not only the case that formal institutions had changed. It was also difficult to make predictions about the future course of institutional change. The politics of the second and third decades of the twentieth century were such that it was necessary for politicians to form coalitions with all kinds of groups—or risk being driven from power by competing factions. Thus, even if a federal or state executive had a probusiness track record, he could not be counted on to enact probusiness policies in the future.

Postrevolutionary Political and Economic Development

Under these conditions of extreme political instability, how was it possible for the government to create commitments to asset holders? Essentially, Mexico's postrevolutionary presidents quickly realized that they would have to follow the same strategy that Díaz had: backward integration into the economic elite, allowing them to shape the policies that affected their interests. They would also have to forward-integrate, allowing political agents to become businessmen. This would mean that members of the government and the private sector would share the same fate, creating a credible

---

23. Maria del Carmen Collado Herrera, *Empresarios y políticos, entre la Restauración y la Revolución 1920–1924* (Mexico City: Instituto Nacional de Estudios Históricos de la Revolución Mexicana, 1996), pp. 138, 250–52, 254, 289.

commitment to not change policies. They also realized, however, that they would have to backward-integrate into at least one other group: organized labor. Díaz had been able to deal with Mexico's workers with the rural police and the army. In the postrevolutionary period, this was simply no longer going to be possible.

Renewed Vertical Political Integration

Mexico's postrevolutionary constitution did little to constrain vertical political integration. As we noted earlier, one feature of vertical political integration is a high degree of authoritarianism. Mexico's 1917 constitution provided, in fact, few constraints on presidents and state governors. Supremacy, at both the state and federal levels, lay with the executive, who could initiate as well as approve legislation. In fact, the federal constitution empowered the president to issue executive orders to enforce sanitary laws, control public expenditures, revoke franchises, forfeit land grants, and expel pernicious foreigners. The president, working through the Permanent Commission of Congress (fourteen senators and fifteen federal deputies who the president played a role in appointing), could depose state governors. The president also had the constitutional prerogative of suspending at any time of public danger or emergency any provision of the Bill of Rights or other guarantees. Finally, and perhaps most fundamentally, the president had the right to issue decrees pending congressional action. Thus, a congress that failed to act on a particular issue could simply be sidestepped by a presidential decree.[24] As one contemporary observed: "Even in the case of necessity for enacting enabling laws putting into effect the constitutional provisions, the power of the President to issue decrees pending congressional action gives him, especially in case of the inability or unwillingness of Congress to pass constructive legisla-

24. Robert Glass Clelland, *The Standard Authority on Mexico* (Los Angeles: Mexican Yearbook Publishing Company, 1922), pp. 101–4.

tion, an autocratic power which militates against stability of government while seeming to increase it temporarily."[25] These provisions were no accident. Backward integration, as a political strategy, is impossible when policymaking is constrained by democratic institutions. This is because decisionmaking under backward integration means that the groups that provide the government with needed support write the rules that govern their activities. If these decisions need to be ratified by an open and elected parliament, then the groups with which the government integrates will be constrained, reducing the rewards from integration. Under conditions of political instability, this would make it difficult for the government to gain the support of economic elites. These groups might decide to commit to another faction that can better guarantee them rents in return for their support. In short, freeing the president from congressional or judicial checks meant that decisions could be made in smoke-filled rooms without worrying about how they would play in the legislature.

Laying out the process of backward and forward integration across the economy in the 1920s is beyond the scope of this chapter. To give readers a sense of what took place, however, we provide below examples from banking, manufacturing, and organized labor.

BANKING.   Throughout the civil war period of the Mexican revolution all sides had engaged in predation against the banking system, resulting by 1917 in the de facto nationalization of most of the banking system and the confiscation of the assets of many of the banks that were not nationalized. After the fighting was over, however, the government's need for revenue remained. At the same time, reconciliation with the private sector was absolutely necessary if the constitucionalists were to reestablish the credibility needed to reopen Mexico's access to credit.

25. Clelland, *Standard Authority*, 1922, pp. 102–3.

Unfortunately, the government was unable to make a credible commitment that it would not engage in predation in the future for four major reasons. First, President Obregón's efforts to reconcile with the bankers were slowed by a banking panic in Mexico City in 1920 that affected the ability of banks to be reopened.[26] Meanwhile, uncertainty over whether Article 27 of the constitution of 1917 allowed banks to own farmland prevented them from making any kind of mortgage loan or loan secured by real property to agricultural interests.[27] Second, the government's financial situation prevented it from making payments on loans obtained through parastatal banks. Also, the government borrowed money from other lenders but lacked the administrative capacity to collect taxes to repay its debts.[28] Third, monetary uncertainty contributed to the banks' unwillingness to lend. Gold coins had been Mexico's primary circulating medium since the end of the hyperinflation, but in late 1921 an unexpected drop in the price of silver caused gold to leave circulation. As a result, the financial pages began quoting silver's discount against gold pesos, and Mexico found itself, in effect, with two currencies whose day-to-day value fluctuated randomly.[29] The fourth and final structural problem was political instability. Rumors continued to proliferate about the stability of President Obregón's regime.

Starting in 1923, Obregón and his successor, Plutarco Elias

---

26. *Boletín Financiero y Minero*, 2/26/21. The financial press attributed the reopening of the Banco Mercantil de Monterrey and Banco de Nuevo León to the fact that both banks had been able to spirit away some resources to the United States in the early stages of the revolution and thus were not as badly affected by the specie seizures. *Boletín Financiero y Minero*, 3/10/21.

27. *Boletín Financiero y Minero*, 3/10/21.

28. Oficio no. 001147 from the chief of the credit department, 2/15/23, *Correspondencia con la SHCP*, vol. 9, AHBNM. The state collected only 90 percent of the assessed value of the taxes. Whether the wedge was retained by the companies or stolen by lower-level officials is not known (most likely both).

29. *Boletín Financiero y Minero*, 12/17/21.

Calles (ruled 1924–28) decided to focus on reestablishing internal credibility by allowing the bankers to write the banking law and irreversibly linking the government to the new structure. In addition to bringing the bankers back into the game, and easing the government's desperate fiscal situation, such measures would also in the long run be a better way to regain access to foreign credit. Rather than repay the foreign debt, they allowed the bankers to write a new banking law, saved oil tax revenues, and created a federally owned bank that irreversibly hitched both the government (as an impersonal entity) and the economic interests of prominent politicians to the preservation of the new rules.

The first move was to follow the example of the Porfiriato and allow the bankers to write a new and favorable banking law. Finance Minister Pani called a national bankers' convention in late 1923, bringing in representatives of both the old Porfirian banks and their newer competitors.[30] Pani conscripted two old Porfirian bankers and politicians, Pablo Macedo and Enrique Creel, to advise the convention. Macedo was a highly placed Banamex board member who had been the president of Congress in the Díaz government. Enrique Creel was a prominent Chihuahua banker, former governor of the state of Chihuahua, founder of the now-defunct Banco Central, and secretary of foreign affairs under Díaz. He was also one of the richest men in the country, the result of three decades in which he and his father-in-law (former governor Luis Terrazas) ran Chihuahua as a personal family business.[31]

Unsurprisingly, the resulting legislation was tailor-made to protect the interests of the existing banks. The new law, enacted in 1925, established high barriers to entry. Banks operating outside the

---

30. Ernesto Lobato Lopez, *El Crédito en México: esbozo histórico hasta 1925* (Mexico City: Fondo de Cultura Economica, 1945), p. 280.

31. Secretaría de Comercio y Fomento Industrial (SCHP), *Comisión Permanente de la Convención Bancaria* (Mexico City, 1924), p. 264–72.

Federal District required a minimum capital investment of a half-million pesos, while those that wished to operate a branch or office in the capital had to invest at least one million pesos before they could open their doors. In addition, no banks could operate without the specific approval of the finance secretary and the president.[32]

The government also pressed ahead with the establishment of a state-owned Single Bank of Issue that would have a monopoly over paper money. President Calles began by ordering, on December 24, 1924, that the receipts from the 10 percent railroad tax and the petroleum tax would henceforth go directly into federal coffers, not Banamex, and he reorganized the newly empowered agency, the Comisión Monetaria, from a federal bureau into a state-owned corporation. This gave the government both a source of finance (the tax receipts) and an organization that could serve as the basis for a bank. Banamex's president, Agustin Legorreta, argued that this violated Mexico's agreements with the International Bankers Committee and that the money freed up by the suppression of the Delahuertista rebellion should go to paying the international debt to no avail.[33]

On January 1, 1925, the government incorporated the Comisión as a bank of discount and deposit.[34] On January 25, 1925, the General Credit Institutions and Banking Establishments Act came into effect.[35] The committee managed the Comisión Monetaria until it accumulated sufficient resources to open its doors as the Banco de México (Banxico) on September 1, 1925. The government immediately ordered Banamex to transfer over all funds and securities held

32. Lobato López, *Crédito en México,* pp. 281–83.

33. Letter from the finance subsecretary, 1/15/25, *Correspondencia con la SHCP,* vol. 11, AHBNM, and ordinary session, 1/21/25, *Actas de Consejo,* vol. 10, AHBNM.

34. Sterrett and Davis, *Fiscal and Economic Condition,* p. 134.

35. Circular no. 3 from the Comisión Nacional Bancaria (CNB), 3/13/25,*Correspondencia con la SHCP,* vol. 11, AHBNM.

as security deposits for contracts with the federal government.[36] Four months later, the government officially transferred the revenues from the oil and railroad taxes to Banxico from Banamex, ending the last of its Porfirian-era special privileges.[37] Other banks also purchased Banxico stock to avail themselves of its rediscount facilities in 1925.[38]

Like its private competitors, Banxico lent heavily and directly to commercial enterprises on the basis of inside connections. President Calles's sugar refinery, the Compañía Azucarera El Mante, for example, received massive infusions of credit.[39] Other politicians and relatives connected with Calles received credit from the new bank. One of President Calles's son-in-laws, Fernando Torreblanca, received large loans, as did Torreblanca's two brothers, Edmundo and Rodolfo. A sugar producer owned by another one of the president's son-in-laws, Jorge Almada, the Compañía Azucarera Almada, took out several long-term loans. Additional credits went to the politicians Moisés and Aaron Sáenz, Secretary of Industry, Commerce, and Labor Luis M. Morones, Finance Secretary Alberto J. Pani, former finance secretary Luis Cabrera, and, of course, former president Alvaro Obregón himself.[40] In this way, Mexican policymakers engaged in both backward and forward integration.

The effect of this, however, was to reestablish a degree of stability. A single institution, in which both major private bankers and prominent federal politicians possessed a substantial stake, dominated lending to the federal government. Further, by making its

36. Ordinary session, 9/17/25, *Actas de Consejo*, vol. 10, AHBNM.

37. Circular 12-10, 1/21/26, *Correspondencia con la SHCP*, vol. 12, AHBNM.

38. Sterrett and Davis, *Fiscal and Economic Condition*, p. 27.

39. See Enrique Krauze, *La Reconstruccion Economica* (Mexico: Colegio de México, 1977), p. 30. Gómez Morín had to resign the presidency of the bank in 1929, partially due to these loans to Calles.

40. Eduardo Turrent Díaz, *Historia del Banco de México* (Mexico City: Banco de Mexico, 1982), p. 162.

rediscount facilities available to the private banks, which therefore became its primary clients, the government increased the credibility of its promise that bankers' property rights would in the future be stable. By running budget surpluses for two years and founding Banxico, the government created more financial stability than would have been possible by continuing to pay the foreign debt. Foreign bondholders, of course, recognized that this meant they would likely never be repaid, but the government correctly judged that they would not be likely to lend more to Mexico regardless.

MANUFACTURING.   Following the revolution of 1910–1917, Mexico's manufacturers not only faced an organized and politically powerful workforce but also faced a government that had the legal ability to reduce their property rights. They faced two practical problems. First, the industrialists had supported the counterrevolutionary government of General Victoriano Huerta against Venustiano Carranza and his allies (at the time, Villa and Zapata). Second, and perhaps even more fundamentally, no government, regardless of its stated ideology, could make a credible commitment to protect business interests. The manufacturers understood that any government that came to power, even if its leaders were businessmen who professed to be probusiness, faced the threat of being overthrown. Any president or state governor who wanted to maintain himself in power would have to invite groups who were antibusiness into a coalition.

Following the constitution of 1917, two major reforms directly affected the property rights of Mexico's manufacturers. The first was a general redefinition of property rights. Article 27 of the constitution of 1917 made the federal government the residual claimant on all property rights. Since private property was created by the government (as a privilege, not an inherent right), the government had the authority to terminate private property in the public interest. The implications were not lost on the country's industrialists, who feared that the government would expropriate their factories. This was a very real threat indeed. The government had already carried out a de facto nationalization of the banking system from 1915 to 1917. Many of the industrialists were, in fact, bankers. The industrialists had also already seen the confiscation of part of the railroads in 1914, the seizure the Compañía de Tranvias (a streetcar company) in order to resolve a labor dispute that same year, and the seizure of the telephone company in 1915.[41]

The second threat to the property rights of the industrialists was the reduction of the tariffs that protected them from foreign competition. Indeed, the two threats to property rights were clearly linked both in the minds of the industrialists and in actual policy. In July 1917, in order to combat inflation, Carranza declared that common cloth with less than 40 threads per square centimeter (which characterized the vast majority of the production of Mexico's cotton textile factories) would be made exempt from all import tariffs. One month later, Carranza amplified this exemption, completely removing the tariff on common cloth with less than 70 threads per square centimeter and lowering the tariff on fine-weave printed cloth to only 25 percent of its former value.[42] These were nontrivial reductions. Prior to the revolution, Mexico had among the highest rates of protection on cotton goods in the world.[43] Without protective tariffs, Mexico's textile industry had no hope of competing against foreign manufacturers.[44] The industrialists of Mexico City re-

41. Mario Ramirez Rancaño, *Burguesia textil y politica en la Revolucion Mexicana* (Mexico City: Instituto de Investigaciones Sociales, Universidad Nacional Autonoma de Mexico, 1987), p. 177.

42. Ramírez Rancaño, *Burguesia textil*, pp. 208–10

43. William A. Graham-Clark, "Cuba, Mexico, and Central America," in William A. Graham-Clark, *Cotton Goods in Latin America, Part 1* (Washington, D.C.: USGPO, 1909), p. 38.

44. On the protection afforded by the tariff, see Beatty, *Industrialization*, pp. 64, 74. On relative costs of production in different countries, see Gregory Clark, "Why

sponded by declaring a lockout, throwing four thousand mill hands out of work. Carranza upped the ante, sending a telegram to every state governor asking for a list of the paralyzed factories and drafting a law, based on Articles 27 and 123 of the constitution, allowing the government to seize control of factories and place them under the administrative direction of the secretary of the treasury, much in the same manner as it had earlier done with the banks. The Chamber of Deputies (Mexico's lower house) approved the law that same day, as did, with some revision, the Senate two months later.[45]

Ultimately, the seizure of the factories was headed off. A delegation of 112 industrialists met with the secretary of industry and commerce throughout November 1917. The industrialists hoped, in fact, to open the Congress of Industrialists with the issue of the tariff but to then move on to attack Articles 27 and 123 of the constitution of 1917. This strategy was only partially successful. The government made it clear that Articles 27 and 123 were nonnegotiable.[46] Mexico's industrialists were simply going to have to live with the labor and property laws that came out of the revolution. The Carranza government also stated that as a general principle it was going to hew to a free trade policy. Yet here the government found some room to maneuver. Although it might in principle be in favor of free trade, it could on an ad hoc basis depart from this policy. Thus did the Carranza government back down on the tariff, restoring the old levels of trade protection.[47] The point had been

---

Isn't the Whole World Developed? Lessons from the Cotton Mills," *Journal of Economic History* 47 (1987): 141–73.

45. Ramírez Rancaño, *Burguesia textil*, pp. 213–17.

46. The government took the position that amendments to the constitution could only be enacted by a vote of two-thirds of the lower house of Congress and a majority of the state legislatures. Neither the government's representative at the Congress, Alberto J. Pani, the minister of industry, commerce and labor, nor the industrialists had the authority to amend the constitution.

47. Ramírez Rancaño, *Burguesia textil*, pp. 227–58; Secretaría de Industria Comercio y Trabajo, pp. 177, 181.

made, however: Mexico's industrialists faced the twin threats of expropriation and downward revisions of the tariff.

Since it was difficult to predict the course of political change in Mexico, there was a high probability that these threats could re-emerge at any time. This unpredictability of government policy was not a distant theoretical abstraction: it was an all too real problem for the industrialists. Although Carranza had backed down in 1917 on the issue of protective tariffs, the fact that the tariff structure was specific (not ad valorum) meant that unless the tariff schedule was regularly revised upward, changes in the exchange rate would grad-ually work to effectively reduce protection. In fact, the coefficient of protection (total tariff revenues divided by the value of all dutiable goods) dropped by nearly 50 percent from 1919 to 1920. As soon as Alvaro Obregón took office after the coup that ousted Carranza, Mexico's major textile manufacturers appealed to him to raise the tariff so that they would not have to close their factories. They were assured that the government would revise import tariffs industry by industry with the goal of assuring the protection of national indus-try. The industrialists had asked for tariff increases in certain classes of goods by as much as 100 percent and thought that they had been promised revisions in the area of 50 percent. When the government published the new tariff schedules, however, the increase was only 10 percent.[48] Thus, the 1921 coefficient of protection was only slightly higher than it had been in 1920—roughly half its 1910 value.[49]

The question of the tariff would continually reemerge through-out the Obregón government. Mexico's industrialists, however, were now organized into the Confederación de Cámaras Indus-

---

48. Collado Herrera, *Empresarios y políticos*, p. 208. They also asked for a decrease in freight rates, a reduction in taxes, and right-to-work laws.

49. Daniel Cosio Villegas, *La Cuestión Arancelaria en México* (Mexico City: Uni-versidad Nacional Autónoma de México, 1989), p. 58.

triales (Concamin), which waged a constant battle for protective tariffs. Each time that an affiliated industry was hurt by foreign competition, representatives of Concamin lobbied the government.[50] Finally, in 1923, the government came to the conclusion that it had to allow the nation's industrialists to make the tariff policies. In that year, Secretary of the Treasury Adolfo de la Huerta extended an invitation to the various industrialist and merchant associations to form technical commissions on the tariff. From the point of view of the factory owners, this was a major victory. The data indicate that beginning in 1923 there was a substantial jump in the level of protection. The coefficient of protection was 24 percent, more than 70 percent above its 1920 value.[51]

ORGANIZED LABOR. The process of backward-integrating with the labor movement—integrating the leaders of the emerging labor organizations into labor policy—was long and slow. As far back as 1915 Carranza had realized the importance of the urban working class and had brought the anarchist-oriented Casa del Obrero Mundial (COM) into his coalition. In return for organizing six Red Battalions to fight Villa and Zapata, the COM was allowed to organize workers in those states under constitutionalist control. This alliance, however, was not long lasting. In 1916 Carranza turned on his former allies, disbanding the Red Battalions and declaring martial law to end a general strike in Mexico City.[52]

Obregón and Calles recognized that they would need to come

50. Collado Herrera, *Empresarios y políticos,* pp. 126, 212.

51. Cosio Villegas, *Cuestión arancelaria,* p. 58. The coefficient of protection then gradually climbed through the end of the decade. At its low point in 1920, it was 14 percent (compared to 30 percent in 1910). By 1923 it was 24 percent, rising to 27 percent in 1927 and to 31 percent in 1928.

52. Kevin J. Middlebrook, *The Paradox of Revolution: Labor, the State, and Authoritarianism in Mexico* (Baltimore: Johns Hopkins University Press, 1995), pp. 18–19.

to a more full accommodation with the labor movement. Labor had continued to organize: by 1918 there were numerous unions, of various ideological orientations, that were organizing into multiple, competing labor federations. The leadership of one of these, the reformist Confederación Regional Obrera Mexicana (CROM), understood that the postrevolutionary governments would need to backward-integrate into the labor movement. The outcome of this integration was that the CROM emerged as a powerful political player throughout the 1920s and was allowed to shape labor law in fundamental ways.

The leader of the CROM, Luis Morones, understood that the path to power in Mexico lay not only in creating a broad-based labor federation but also in federalizing labor law and building a political movement that could then effectively influence decisions at the federal level. Thus, within a year of its founding in 1918, the CROM organized a political party, the Partido Laborista Mexicano. In that same year, the CROM struck a secret deal with General Obregón that it would mobilize support for him in the 1920 presidential elections in exchange for privileged political access, the creation of a separate labor ministry (which the CROM would control), and presidential support for federalized labor law codifying Article 123 of the constitution.[53]

With the outbreak of the de la Huerta rebellion in 1923, the CROM's influence grew rapidly. The CROM had played an important role in helping Obregón win the presidency in 1920. Its support of Calles and Obregón against de la Huerta, and its crucial support of Calles's presidential election in 1924, earned it tremendous influence in the federal government. Luis Morones was, in fact, made secretary of industry, commerce, and labor from 1924 to 1928. The CROM-PLM also built a powerful delegation in Congress. In 1926, at the height of its electoral power, it held 11 of 58 positions in the

53. Middlebrook, *Paradox of Revolution*, p. 77.

Senate and 40 of 272 seats in the federal Chamber of Deputies. Indeed, Morones held presidential aspirations, hoping to receive Calles's support for a presidential bid in 1928. Only the strong resistance of conservative elements in the army headed this off.

These political connections, in turn, strengthened the CROM's organizational strength. It used the positions it controlled in the government to enforce dues deductions from the salaries of federal employees, which was a major source of financial support. In addition, the ability of the CROM to control appointments to state-level arbitration boards, coupled with the influence of its elected officials, meant that the CROM could force employers to recognize CROM-affiliated unions at the same time that it undermined rival non-CROM unions. Indeed, the fact that the secretary of industry, commerce, and labor could rule a strike illegal (which, in turn allowed employers to fire the workforce and hire replacements) gave Morones a very powerful tool against rival labor unions or federations.[54]

From the point of view of both Obregón and Calles, and from the point of view of Mexico's employers, the CROM was the best alternative in the new world of Mexican labor relations. The revolution had brought to the fore a number of labor organizations, many of them far more militantly anticapitalist than Morones and the CROM. Indeed, the CROM had a fundamentally reformist ideology. It did not so much want to overthrow capitalism as it wanted to win labor its share of the economic growth that Morones believed was in Mexico's immediate future.[55] Morones, it should be pointed out, also wanted to win for himself a share of payments from unions

54. Middlebrook, *Paradox of Revolution*, pp. 79–80.
55. For discussions of the CROM's ideology, see Jean Meyer, Enrique Krauze, and Cayetano Reyes, *Historia de la Revolución Mexicana, 1924–1928: 11 Estado y sociedad con Calles* (Mexico: El Colegio de México, 1977), pp. 83–84; Enrique Krauze, Jean Meyer, and Cayetano Reyes, *Historia de la Revolución Mexicana, 1924–1928: 10 La reconstrucción económica* (Mexico: El Colegio de México, 1977), pp. 183–91.

and employers that the CROM extracted through various corrupt schemes.

This is not to say, however, that labor peace was achieved in Mexico under the CROM. The coalition of Morones, Calles, and Obregón fell apart over the presidential succession of 1928 when Calles engineered Obregón's reelection over the objection of Morones and other CROM leaders. Morones and other CROM leaders were therefore charged with having played a role in the assassination of Obregón in 1928, and were forced to resign their positions in the Calles administration. Over the next several years, Morones would make other strategic blunders, including refusing to cooperate with Calles over his efforts to build the Partido Revolucionario Nacional, preferring to preserve the PLM as an independent party. The result was that the first of the three puppet presidents controlled by Calles (Portes Gil) worked to undermine the CROM by removing CROM members from federal jobs, removing CROM members from Juntas de Conciliación y Arbitraje, and using the army against CROM unions in worker-employer conflicts.[56]

Thus, by the early 1930s the attempt to backward-integrate into the labor movement through the CROM had failed. There were, once again, multiple competing organizations that all vied for political influence. In the end, President Lazaro Cárdenas (ruled 1934–40) successfully backward-integrated into organized labor by formally integrating the Confederación de Trabajadores Mexicanos, a broad-based labor federation that even included some labor leaders who had cut their teeth in the CROM, into the newly created corporatist party, the Partido de la Revolución Mexicana. That successful process of backward integration, however, was long and slow. It was not until 1938 that Cárdenas created the PRM.

Political development eventually converged to a structure similar to the Porfiriato's. At the end of the revolutionary period, politi-

---

56. Middlebrook, *Paradox of Revolution*, p. 81.

cal institutions once again centralized power around the presidency. A new stable political equilibrium finally emerged in the mid-1930s under President Lázaro Cárdenas, who transformed the PNR (a party founded by Calles in 1929) from a talking shop designed to distribute spoils among a few leaders into a genuine corporatist party and, in many ways, a branch of the federal government, completing the integration process begun by President Obregón. This required Cárdenas to arm leagues of workers and peasants, carry out a sweeping agrarian reform, encourage the growth of unions, and deport Calles to Los Angeles. The structure that finally emerged remained stable until the 1980s, and the distinction between party and government has remained vague in Mexico until this very day. There were three differences, however, between the post-Cárdenas equilibrium and the Porfiriato: more social groups (such as workers and peasants or at least their representatives) were integrated into the system; forward integration (the movement of politicians into lucrative private activities) had become more prevalent, especially through the direct participation of state-owned institutions in the economy; and there was now a credible selection mechanism by which a president appointed his successor and then permanently and completely retired from the political arena. Although we do not discount the importance of these changes, the basic Porfirian game remained intact, and Mexico regained stability in 1934–88 under conditions similar to those that had prevailed in 1876–1911.

Economic Performance

Our current research involves the analysis of extensive data sets from various sectors of the Mexican economy during its revolutionary years. Providing a detailed discussion of how the process of vertical integration affected economic performance across the Mexican economy is beyond the scope of this chapter. In order to provide readers with a sense of the economic outcomes of vertical integration, we discuss the evolution of investment and production in the manufacturing sector.[57] We note, however, that we also gathered data on banking, mining, petroleum extraction, and agriculture.

INVESTMENT. We have been able to retrieve data on new capacity or investment in the cement, steel, and cotton textile industries. We have also retrieved detailed data on exports of industrial machinery from the United States and the United Kingdom to Mexico, which is an excellent measure of aggregate new investment because virtually all of Mexico's capital goods had to be imported.

Productive capacity in the cement industry continued to expand both during and after the revolution, growing from 66,000 metric tons a year in 1906 to 151,000 in 1910, 177,000 in 1912, 222,000 in 1920, and 246,000 in 1928. This rate of growth in capacity is especially impressive in light of the fact that capacity utilization was almost always less than 60 percent, implying that the owners of firms were confident enough about the future to invest well ahead of demand (see table 2.1).[58]

Data on the nation's integrated steel producing monopolist, Fundidora Monterrey, tell a similar story. During the years of military conflict, Fundidora Monterrey closed its doors and spent no

57. We have provided a more detailed analysis of the manufacturing sector in Stephen Haber and Armando Razo, "Political Instability and Economic Performance: Evidence from Revolutionary Mexico," *World Politics* 51 (1998): 99–143. This chapter incorporates, however, new data on machinery investment and production inputs, which corroborate our previous research.

58. The fact that firms invested ahead of demand is explained by the fact that cement production tends, most everywhere in the world, to be characterized by local monopolies. The high bulk-to-price ratio of cement means that it is economical to ship it only over short distances. In order to expand, therefore, firms must erect new production facilities in new areas of the country. Firms also tend to erect more productive capacity than they need in these new markets in order to keep out potential rivals. See Ronald N. Johnson and Allen Parkman, "Spatial Monopoly, Non-Zero Profits, and Entry Deterrence: The Case of Cement," *Review of Economics and Statistics* 65 (1983): 431–39.

TABLE 2.1

Capacity and Output in Mexico's Cement Industry, 1906–1938
(In thousands of metric tons)

Year	Capacity	Output	Capacity Utilization (in percent)
1906	66	20	30%
1907	66	30	45
1908	66	40	61
1909	86	50	58
1910	151	60	40
1911	152	50	33
1912	177	40	23
1913	177	30	17
1914	177	25	14
1915	177	10	6
1916	177	20	11
1917	177	30	17
1918	177	40	23
1919	177	40	23
1920	222	45	20
1921	222	50	23
1922	222	70	32
1923	222	90	41
1924	222	107	48
1925	222	110	50
1926	222	151	68
1927	222	158	71
1928	246	204	83
1929	291	158	54
1930	291	227	78
1931	375	157	42
1932	405	138	34
1933	405	173	43
1934	405	241	60
1935	405	252	62
1936	405	286	71
1937	405	345	85
1938	513	374	73

SOURCE: Stephen H. Haber, *Industry and Underdevelopment: The Industrialization of Mexico, 1890–1940* (Stanford: Stanford University Press, 1989), pp. 41, 127, 165, 177.

funds on plant and equipment. As soon as normalcy returned, however, the firm invested in a dramatic fashion: the value of its physical plant grew 41 percent from 1919 to 1921, even in the face of a rate of capacity utilization of less than 40 percent (see table 2.2).

Other industries show similar patterns. As table 2.3 indicates, the cotton textiles industry, measured in spindlage, declined by 25 percent from 1913 to 1917.[59] Much of this loss was clearly produced by firms temporarily closing their doors during the worst phases of the fighting. Indeed, the only way to explain a 28 percent jump in capacity from 1917 to 1919 is that firms that had closed their doors during the years of civil war reopened them as soon as military conflict ended. The recovery went well beyond the reopening of old capacity, however. New plants and equipment were being purchased as well. In fact, in 1921 the cotton textile industry was 10 percent larger than it had been in 1910 (and roughly equal to its 1913 level), and in the four years from 1921 to 1925 the industry grew an additional 9 percent, making it 20 percent larger than it had been in 1910. This increase in industry capacity cannot be explained as the result of population growth. The Mexican population was 5 percent smaller in 1921 than it had been in 1910.[60] In short, the data do not support the hypothesis that the revolution discouraged new investment over the medium term. The textile industry was larger in per capita terms after the revolution than before the revolution.

The patterns displayed by the cotton textile, steel, and cement industries are corroborated by data on U.S. and British exports of

59. Spindles constitute the most important capital input for the production of cotton textile goods, and thus the literature tends to use spindlage as the measure of capital or capacity. See, for example, Nancy F. Kane, *Textiles in Transition: Technology, Wages, and Industry Relocation in the U.S. Textile Industry* (Westport, Conn.: Greenwood, 1988).

60. Mexican population data are from Instituto Nacional de Estadística Geografia e Informática, *Estadísticas Históricas de México* (Mexico: INEGI, 1994), p. 44.

TABLE 2.2

Capacity, Output, and Value of Physical Plant in Fundidora Monterrey
(Mexico's steel monopolist)

Year	Capacity [a]	Output [b]	Capacity Utilization (in percent)	Value of Physical Plant [c]
1903	110	22	20%	8,388
1904	110	36	33	9,236
1905	110	4	4	9,833
1906	110	25	23	10,032
1907	110	16	15	9,526
1908	110	17	15	9,082
1909	110	59	54	9,317
1910	110	45	41	9,365
1911	110	71	65	9,087
1912	110	33	30	9,337
1913	110	12	11	9,226
1914	110	0	0	8,989
1915	110	0	0	8,509
1916	110	0	0	8,161
1917	110	12	11	7,819
1918	110	21	19	7,830
1919	110	21	19	7,374
1920	110	15	14	9,133
1921	110	42	38	10,421
1922	110	24	22	10,217
1923	110	44	40	10,238
1924	110	19	17	10,340
1925	110	49	45	9,872
1926	110	62	56	9,700
1927	110	41	37	9,436
1928	110	51	46	9,173
1929	110	60	55	8,679
1930	110	58	53	8,649
1931	110	53	48	8,124
1932	110	20	18	7,625
1933	110	54	49	7,528
1934	110	66	60	6,530
1935	110	64	58	6,882
1936	110	88	80	7,450
1937	110	59	54	8,868

[a] Capacity of the blast furnace, in thousands of metric tons.

[b] Output of the blast furnace, in thousands of metric tons.

[c] Book value of the physical plant (land, equipment, buildings), net of depreciation in thousands of pesos. Physical plant depreciated at flat rate of 5 percent per annum.

SOURCE: Calculated from Fundidora Monterrey, *Informe Annual*, 1900–1938.

TABLE 2.3
Mexican Cotton Textile Industry, 1883–1933

Year	Estimated Nominal Value Output [a,c]	Estimated Real Value Output [a,c]	Estimated Meters of Output [a]	Estimated Spindles	Estimated Worker Equivalents [b]
1883	11,484	8,538	76,331		
1888 [d]	264	216	60,842	249,561	15,083
1889	10,909	8,942	83,827		
1891	12,066	9,891	93,527	277,784	14,051
1893	19,064	15,628	122,550	370,570	21,963
1895	23,554	21,222	170,929	411,090	18,208
1896	23,658	23,658	206,412	430,868	19,771
1899	29,753	29,753	231,686	491,443	23,731
1900	35,459	35,459	261,397	588,474	27,767
1901	33,877	33,877	262,044	591,506	26,709
1902	28,780	28,780	235,956	595,728	24,964
1903	36,907	36,907	262,170	632,601	26,149
1904	42,511	42,511	280,710	635,940	27,456
1905	51,214	51,214	310,692	678,058	30,162
1906	51,171	51,171	349,712	688,217	31,673
1907	51,686	51,686	428,284	613,548	33,132
1908	54,934	54,934	368,370	732,876	35,816
1909	43,370	43,370	314,228	726,278	32,229
1910	50,651	50,651	315,322	702,874	31,963
1911	51,348	51,348	341,441	725,297	32,147
1912	63,802	72,834	319,668	762,149	32,209
1913	54,002	33,978	298,897	752,804	32,641
1917 [e]	25,125	12,266		573,092	22,187
1918	48,567	15,111	180,453	689,173	23,067
1919	80,781	23,333	305,509	735,308	21,877
1920	120,492	27,840	298,829	753,837	24,691
1921	93,342	66,826	338,346	770,945	25,485
1922	85,023	53,040	330,601	803,230	26,451
1923	97,563	44,214	303,090	802,363	26,419
1924	96,435	44,155	285,594	812,165	25,155
1925	102,527	56,839	380,041	840,890	33,262
1926	88,766	60,562	327,487	832,193	27,476
1927	73,179	51,156	308,940	821,211	27,492
1928	89,630	52,529	300,425	823,862	25,348
1929	105,055	67,861	389,147	839,100	27,598

TABLE 2.3

(*continued*)

Year	Estimated Nominal Value Output [a,c]	Estimated Real Value Output [a,c]	Estimated Meters of Output [a]	Estimated Spindles	Estimated Worker Equivalents [b]
1930	84,876	58,426	305,512	803,873	27,729
1931	78,580	70,154	269,085	838,223	25,788
1932	88,694	52,333	301,537	851,163	25,223
1933	110,612	47,569	381,783	862,303	27,308

[a] Output reported in thousands.

[b] Number of workers adjusted for changes in the length of the workday: 12 hours from 1850 to 1913, 10 hours from 1914 to 1917, 8 hours from 1918 to 1933.

[c] Value of output calculated from prices and quantities. This is a lower-bounded estimate since not all quantities were matched with a respective price.

[d] For this year, the majority of firms reported output in meters.

[e] Spindles and workers data for 1917 were taken from *Estadísticas Históricas* (fn. 27), 616.

SOURCE: Stephen H. Haber and Armando Razo, "Political Instability and Economic Performance: Evidence from Revolutionary Mexico," *World Politics* 51 (1998): 99–143.

industrial machinery to Mexico. In table 2.4 we present estimates of the real value of exports of industrial machinery from these two countries to Mexico. We break down industrial machines into three broad categories: steam engines, boilers, and their parts; textile machinery; and manufacturing machinery other than textiles. All of the series indicate the same pattern: new investment, as measured by the export of industrial machinery to Mexico, did not decline during the early years of political instability. Moreover, by 1920, every category of industrial machinery exported from the United States and Great Britain to Mexico had surpassed its Porfirian levels. In fact, during the 1920s industrial machinery exports to Mexico were anywhere from two (in the case of textile machines) to six times (manufacturing machines other than textiles) what they had been during the decade before the revolution.

The data on exports of industrial machinery to Mexico indicate that firms were doing much more than undertaking incremental

TABLE 2.4

Combined U.S./U.K. Machinery Exports to Mexico, 1900–1935 (in 1929 U.S. dollars)

| Year | Agricultural | Steam Engines, Boilers, and Pipes and Fittings | MANUFACTURING | | | Petroleum and Mining | Unspecified Machinery | Grand Total of Machinery Exports |
			Industrial Machinery	Textile Machinery	Total Manufacturing			
1900	393,363	651,490	266,655	468,115	1,386,260	104,509	396,328	2,280,852
1901	331,248	569,966	218,603	183,564	972,134	101,772	264,131	1,669,374
1902	293,125	705,417	138,589	248,021	1,092,026	134,496	271,688	1,792,216
1903	247,077	747,508	373,789	147,243	1,268,541	184,307	189,653	1,889,579
1904	227,542	642,555	393,401	395,789	1,431,745	245,282	182,888	2,087,867
1905	226,056	675,932	625,306	265,632	1,566,870	408,306	178,529	2,380,750
1906	357,254	1,554,324	803,813	354,592	2,712,729	665,152	277,606	4,013,837
1907	365,827	1,546,928	1,002,979	471,916	3,021,822	2,886,603	455,571	6,735,690
1908	305,907	1,552,717	968,387	472,963	2,994,067	2,073,626	249,996	5,652,814
1909	269,825	1,745,211	629,118	525,028	2,899,356	1,720,168	192,055	5,089,955
1910	321,341	2,473,655	667,517	349,919	3,491,091	1,798,508	282,808	5,914,464
1911	525,127	1,415,846	1,041,324	331,188	2,788,357	1,852,085	275,940	5,455,835
1912	559,485	1,378,297	719,897	391,488	2,489,682	1,578,034	240,120	4,885,712
1913	654,565	1,667,428	1,416,650	25,922	3,110,000	1,705,669	292,705	5,780,186
1914	182,425	1,324,538	294,144	6,274	1,624,956	1,549,483	64,924	3,427,204
1915	99,609	399,702	112,255	3,405	515,363	440,971	15,535	1,074,022

1916	173,238	849,200	419,905	8,521	1,277,626	677,485	22,448	2,151,537
1917	428,930	2,488,976	859,726	35,552	3,384,254	1,318,772	44,258	5,187,173
1918	1,434,238	115,871	1,457,912	85,800	1,659,582	8,982,030	11,006	12,087,080
1919	2,527,737	11,025,273	2,727,192	164,364	13,916,829	11,001,582	64,200	27,565,106
1920	3,814,471	28,350,017	4,503,392	457,035	33,310,444	18,425,214	1,191,062	56,847,017
1921	2,187,013	1,118,589	3,917,214	138,966	5,174,770	10,379,876	1,284,034	19,083,075
1922	1,632,982	3,544,176	1,666,927	1,112,938	6,324,042	4,863,807	823,143	13,666,864
1923	1,188,473	3,598,330	1,454,173	595,872	5,648,376	5,304,495	196,306	12,381,643
1924	1,563,969	3,539,853	1,377,192	634,439	5,551,485	5,938,456	185,976	13,316,491
1925	2,120,850	3,614,478	1,782,672	916,903	6,314,053	6,348,032	—	14,810,519
1926	2,061,895	2,375,880	6,187,387	1,111,451	9,674,717	5,158,955	—	17,049,447
1927	1,481,988	2,080,808	5,538,085	1,066,284	8,685,178	3,799,112	—	14,076,166
1928	1,766,467	1,782,763	5,139,867	1,123,659	8,046,289	4,389,368	—	14,220,113
1929	2,309,384	2,992,974	7,934,877	680,932	11,608,782	4,289,753	209,148	18,558,819
1930	3,757,625	1,827,263	7,535,382	643,881	10,006,526	2,592,524	156,161	16,622,034
1931	945,699	1,076,060	662,389	426,688	2,165,137	1,280,676	104,233	4,619,725
1932	209,864	495,831	383,290	163,623	1,042,744	846,501	59,869	2,212,686
1933	378,016	531,747	541,879	415,211	1,488,836	1,220,977	65,315	3,255,518
1934	956,451	1,258,459	889,020	532,113	2,679,591	2,424,091	108,017	6,254,033
1935	1,550,738	1,351,441	1,084,168	694,107	3,129,716	2,060,144	114,837	7,050,051

SOURCES: United States: U.S. Department of Commerce, *The Foreign Commerce and Navigation of the United States, 1902–1930*. (Price deflator is the wholesale price index.) United Kingdom: *Annual Statements of the Trade of the United Kingdom with Foreign Countries, 1900–1935*.

increases in productive capacity: the flow of new machinery to Mexico after the revolution exceeded the levels attained before the revolution. Also, new firms entered the market for manufactures both during the revolution and afterward, even in the face of the failure of older, more established firms. Even during the worst years of violent conflict new firms opened their factory gates.[61] There was also new entry in a number of industries by new, large, capital-intensive firms in the early 1920s. In the tobacco industry, for example, the British-American Tobacco Company established two subsidiary manufacturing plants in Mexico that dwarfed their Mexican competitors and quickly drove them out of business.[62]

PRODUCTION.   In our previous work, we have shown that few firms were destroyed or forced into bankruptcy by the revolution.[63] One implication is that production should have quickly regained its Porfirian levels once normalcy returned to the transportation and monetary systems. Two bodies of evidence support this hypothesis. First, we have retrieved evidence on output in the steel, cement, cotton textile, and beer industries. The data for all four industries indicate that there were dramatic declines in production during the violent phase of the revolution, followed by a rapid recovery once the fighting stopped (see tables 2.1, 2.2, 2.3, and 2.5). By the early 1920s production in most industries had surpassed Porfirian levels.

Second, data on electric power generation in Mexico City for commercial light and power uses (the data exclude power generated for the water and tramway systems and for public lighting) point to the same conclusion. (Since the vast majority of Mexican manufacturing at this point operated with electric machinery, commercial

61. Haber and Razo, *Political Instability*, p. 131.
62. Haber, *Industry and Underdevelopment*, pp. 143–44; Sterrett and Davis, *Fiscal and Economic Condition*, p. 208.
63. Haber and Razo, *Political Instability*, pp. 112–19.

TABLE 2.5

Mexican Beer Production, National and Cervecería Cuauhtemoc
(in thousands of liters)

Year	Cervecería Cuauhtemoc	National Output	Cuauhtemoc Market Share (in percent)
1900	4,866	—	—
1901	4,685	—	—
1902	5,581	—	—
1903	5,925	—	—
1904	6,865	—	—
1905	8,884	—	—
1906	13,344	—	—
1907	14,005	—	—
1908	11,183	—	—
1909	11,582	—	—
1910	13,275	—	—
1911	14,172	—	—
1912	16,519	—	—
1913	11,732	—	—
1914–15 [a]	3,359	—	—
1916	2,758	—	—
1917	4,640	—	—
1918	4,977	—	—
1919	7,735	—	—
1920	14,929	—	—
1921	16,689	—	—
1922	13,156	—	—
1923	12,335	—	—
1924	11,564	52,003	22%
1925	15,736	53,673	29
1926	21,521	67,925	32
1927	23,201	71,613	32
1928	22,229	67,911	33
1929	23,174	71,973	32
1930	21,760	72,065	30
1931	18,894	54,711	35
1932	14,367	42,470	34
1933	19,082	52,991	36
1934	24,305	67,368	36
1935	29,291	82,513	35
1936	36,355	98,893	37
1937	44,225	120,805	37
1938	43,483	129,802	33
1939	49,052	160,452	31
1940	54,709	179,198	31

[a] Combined year.

SOURCE: Unpublished data from Cerveceria Cuauhtemoc Sales Department; Direccion General de Estadistica, *Anuario Estadistico de la Republica Mexicana* (Mexico City, 1942), p. 958.

power consumption is a good proxy for industrial activity.) Table 2.6 shows data from the Mexican Light and Power Company indicating a steady rise in commercial power usage from 1907 through the early years of the revolution (peaking in 1912). Power usage declined dramatically from 1912 to 1915 (falling by roughly 40 percent over three years) and then recovered rapidly. By 1917 commercial power consumption in Mexico City was 17 percent higher than in 1910 and continued climbing throughout the 1920s. By 1927, commercial power consumption in Mexico City was three times what it had been on the eve of the revolution.

Concluding Remarks

This chapter has made a substantive argument, based on new theory and evidence, that political instability does not necessarily have a negative impact on economic performance. Our analysis began with a widely accepted premise about the political foundations of growth: governments need to make credible commitments to the protection of private property rights. An emerging consensus claims that credible commitments are impossible to make on the basis of codified institutions. This claim is partly true if we restrict consideration of credible commitment mechanisms to those provided by institutional changes that formally limit the scope (and predatory behavior) of governments. It is an incomplete claim, however, because it ignores the possibility that credible commitments could be made through other mechanisms. We thus propose an alternate theory of governance structures based on vertical political integration, which allows for the possibility of creating credible commitments even under political instability. Our analysis is more general than the existing focus on limited governments. In particular, it suggests that the current focus on the existence of either limited governments (which can sustain growth) versus predatory governments (which hamper growth) is limited because it ignores the fact

TABLE 2.6
*Power Generated by the Mexican Light and Power Company
for Commercial Purposes, 1907–1927*

Year	Thousands of Kilowatt Hours	Index (1910 = 100)
1907	45,779	80
1908	44,061	77
1909	47,074	82
1910	57,112	100
1911	59,244	104
1912	67,565	118
1913	62,117	109
1914	56,274	99
1915	39,096	68
1916	42,888	75
1917	67,062	117
1918	72,901	128
1919	82,212	144
1920	91,145	160
1921	88,379	155
1922	103,111	181
1923	113,704	199
1924	125,424	220
1925	144,230	253
1926	166,483	292
1927	178,089	312

SOURCE: Joseph E. Sterrett and Joseph S. Davis, *The Fiscal and Economic Condition of Mexico: Report Submitted to the International Committee of Bankers on Mexico* (New York: N.p., 1928), p. 213.

that commitment is a matter of degree. Rather than a binary choice, establishing credible commitments is a problem of selecting a particular governance structure from a continuum of different degrees of commitment that a political system can sustain. In fact, limited and predatory governments are but two extreme cases of political structures that integrate private and public interests.

To be sure, these credible commitment mechanisms are clearly a second-best solution and have associated inefficiencies and negative results. On the other hand, there are some advantages of vertical integration relative to a limited government solution. First, vertical integration is feasible under a larger set of conditions. Both empirical evidence and theoretical considerations show us that limited governments are hard to come by even under stable conditions. The conditions for limited government are even more stringent under political instability because governments need to establish credible commitments under severe uncertainty about the resolution of instability. Whereas it is impossible for limited governments to emerge from political instability, we have shown that it is feasible (and indeed expected) for governance structures to establish credible commitments through vertical integration. It should be noted that credible commitments need not be, and often are not, offered to all members of society. In terms of growth, a governance structure that provides protection to elite economic groups is sufficient to sustain economic growth.

This chapter has also provided empirical evidence to test two contending hypotheses about the impact of political instability on economic growth. The first hypothesis, which reflects an emerging consensus among students of the political economy of growth, is that instability should have a negative impact on growth. The second hypothesis, derived from our theory, is that growth can be sustained even under conditions of political instability. We consider a canonical case of political instability, revolutionary Mexico, which provides strong evidence in favor of our hypothesis. On the one hand, the data we have gathered makes a strong case for the continuity (and even improved performance) of the Mexican economy during its revolutionary years. Moreover, our analysis has also shown that the necessary credible commitments by governments came through governance structures that integrated elite economic groups (providing these with special protection and rents).

The Evolution of Suffrage Institutions in the New World: A Preliminary Look

It has long been recognized that the conduct of elections, including who holds the right to vote, is one of the most crucial of institutions. Varying the rules or organization of how votes are cast and of who casts them can have a fundamental impact on the policy choices that the elected representatives—who in some sense constitute the collective government—make. In so doing, there are often major implications for how a society's resources or wealth are distributed across the population, as well perhaps for the pace of economic growth. Given what is at stake, it should not be surprising that throughout history many have fought and died over both the design of the rules and the outcomes of elections.

In recent years there has been an increased appreciation of how democratic rules for electing government representatives might contribute to different paths of development. A number of specific mechanisms have been identified. Many scholars have emphasized the relation between degree of democracy, or the distribution of political influence, and the distribution of income, with reference to how a broader extension of the franchise would lead to different types of tax systems, provisions of public services, legal and regulatory frameworks, levels of corruption, and trade policies than would regimes based on greater concentration of political influence.[1] At least implicit in these treatments have been suggestions that policies with effects on distribution might have indirect consequences on the prospects for long-term economic growth as well. Some have focused on potential negative consequences, such as the disincentives for investment that are created by progressive or higher rates of taxation, or by other infringements on insecure property rights to the streams of income from investments. Where an economic elite wields highly disproportionate political power, or a political elite exploits its position for economic advantage, a broadening of political influence through an extension of the franchise might diminish the returns to members of the elite and dampen their rates of investment.[2] On the other hand, there could well be advantages for growth to having a more equal distribution of political influence. Many would expect, for example, more substantial support of infrastructure and other public goods and services (that would augment the returns to investment by segments of the population outside the elite), a reduction in levels of corruption, and perhaps more competition throughout the economy (with associated improvements in the allocation of resources and in transactions costs).[3]

1. Alexis de Tocqueville, *Democracy in America*, trans. George Lawrence, ed. J. P. Mayer (Garden City, N.Y.: Doubleday, 1969). For other more recent examples of a vast literature, see Daron Acemoglu and James A. Robinson, "Why Did Western Europe Extend the Franchise?" working paper, Massachuetts Institute of Technology and University of California, Berkeley, 2000; Robert J. Barro, *Determinants of Economic Growth* (Cambridge, England: Cambridge University Press, 1997); and Roberto Perotti, "Growth, Income Distribution, and Democracy," *Journal of Economic Growth* 1 (1996): 149–87.

2. Alberto F. Alesina and Dani Rodrik, "Distributive Politics and Economic Growth," *Quarterly Journal of Economics* 109 (1994): 465–90; and Torsten Perrson and Guido Tabellini, "Is Inequality Harmful for Growth? Theory and Evidence," *American Economic Review* 84 (1994): 600–21.

3. Acemoglu and Robinson, "Why Did Western Europe Extend the Franchise?"; Roland Benabou, "Unequal Societies: Income Distribution and the Social

Most of the systematic analysis on how the distribution of political power affects the patterns of growth has been confined to our experience over the late–twentieth century.[4] This work has made important contributions to our knowledge, but there has been relatively little investigation of earlier periods (largely because of the lack of comparable data). One of the problems associated with the focus on the modern record is that examinations of processes that take place over the long run are hampered. A central example of this deficiency is the difficulty of studying where institutions like those that establish the distribution of political power come from. We may all agree that institutions have an impact on growth, but our interpretation of this relationship will vary with our understanding of where institutions come from; in particular, to what extent are institutions exogenous and to what extent are they endogenous (and with respect to which conditions and processes).

This chapter is intended to make a modest contribution toward the goal of improving our knowledge of where institutions have come from by surveying how the rules governing the extension of suffrage, a measure of the distribution of political power, have differed across the countries of North and South America and evolved over time within them. Because of the enormous shocks to these societies associated with European colonization of the New World, and because of the substantial variation among them in their initial characteristics and outcomes, such an examination has the potential for improving our understanding of the conditions that over the long run give rise to more democratic

---

Contract," *American Economic Review* 90 (2000): 96–129; and Gilles Saint-Paul and Thierry Verdier, "Education, Democracy, and Growth," *Journal of Development Economics* 42 (1993): 399–407.

4. The construction and maintenance of a rich cross-country data set for this period has been an enormous boon to scholars in this area. See Robert Summers and Alan Heston, "The Penn World Table (Mark 5): An Expanded Set of International Comparisons, 1950–1988," *Quarterly Journal of Economics* 106 (1991): 327–68.

political institutions. Moreover, it should also allow us a better chance to get at the underlying processes that relate the degree of political democracy or equality to the evolution of strategic economic institutions and to economic development more generally.

That there was extreme variation across the New World in the evolution of social and economic institutions cannot be doubted. Over the sixteenth through the eighteenth centuries, the Europeans had established colonies throughout the Americas as part of a worldwide effort to economically exploit underpopulated or under-defended territories. Nations and private agents set about extracting material and other advantages from unfamiliar types of environments, and there was great diversity in the characteristics of the societies that evolved and their institutions. Common to all of the New World colonies was a high marginal product of labor and, for that era, per capita income. One crucial dimension in which they differed, however, was in the extent of inequality in the distributions of income and human capital, as well as in the homogeneity of the population more generally.[5]

Stanley Engerman and I have previously argued that the substantial variation in the initial degrees of inequality can be largely attributed to factor endowments broadly conceived.[6] Extreme inequality arose in the colonies of the Caribbean and in Brazil because

5. For excellent surveys of the early development of the colonies in the New World, see David W. Galenson, "The Settlement and Growth of the Colonies: Population, Labor, and Economic Development," in Stanley L. Engerman and Robert E. Gallman, eds., *The Cambridge Economic History of the United States*, vol. I, *The Colonial Period* (Cambridge, England: Cambridge University Press, 1995); and James Lockhart and Stuart B. Schwartz, *Early Latin America: A History of Colonial Spanish America and Brazil* (Cambridge, England: Cambridge University Press, 1983).

6. Stanley L. Engerman and Kenneth L. Sokoloff, "Factor Endowments, Institutions, and Differential Paths of Growth among New World Economies: A View from Economic Historians of the United States," in Stephen Haber, ed., *How Latin America Fell Behind* (Stanford: Stanford University Press, 1997).

their soils and climates gave them a comparative advantage in growing sugar and other lucrative crops that were produced at lowest cost on large slave plantations. With the consequent importation of enormous numbers of slaves, their populations came to be composed of a small elite of European descent with the dominant share of the population consisting of slaves, or (later) freedmen, and their descendants. Extreme inequality in wealth and human capital came to characterize much of Spanish America as well. The inequality arose here from the extensive populations of Native Americans and the Spanish practices (significantly influenced by preexisting Native-American organizations in Mexico and Peru) of awarding claims on land, native labor, and rich mineral resources to members of the elite (whose number were limited by restrictive immigration policies), but some societies, such as Argentina, Uruguay, and Costa Rica, were perhaps less affected. In contrast, the societies of the northern part of North America developed with relative equality and population homogeneity, as there were relatively few Native Americans and the climates and soils favored a regime of mixed farming centered on grains and livestock which exhibited limited economies of scale in production.

Contemporary estimates indicating that Latin America has, as a region, the greatest degree of income inequality in the world today make it clear that the extreme disparities of the colonial era have persisted over the long run.[7] Engerman and I have hypothesized that inequality in political influence may have been a powerful contributor to the maintenance of this condition and that such inequality in political power was rooted in the exceptional economic inequality and population heterogeneity that prevailed during the early histories of these societies. Our logic is that to the extent that elites in any society were able to obtain disproportionate political

7. Klaus Deininger and Lyn Squire, "A New Data Set and Measure of Income Inequality," *World Bank Economic Review* 10 (1996): 565–91.

leverage, their efforts could shape legal frameworks and other state policies so as to advantage them relative to others in terms of access to economic and other opportunities. What some have called *political cronyism* would have privileged the individuals in question, as well as their families and children, and encouraged the persistence of inequality—relative to what would transpire in a society that began with relative equality. What was in the private interests of members of the elite may not have been conducive to the growth of the overall economy, however.

What follows shows that the early patterns of the extension of the franchise, the proportions of the respective populations voting, and other aspects of the conduct of elections are generally consistent with the notion that the extent of initial inequality and population heterogeneity was indeed associated—even within the United States and across the nations of Latin America—with the nature of the political institutions that evolved. Specifically, where there was extreme inequality and/or heterogeneity, the proportion of the population that had the right to vote was generally lower, and the timing of the extensions of this right from elite groups to a broad population generally later, than in areas where there was relative homogeneity in the population. These relationships are all the more striking because most of the New World societies were at least nominal democracies by the middle of the nineteenth century and seemed to have embraced the rhetoric of revolution and modernization during their respective movements for independence. Only a few, however, would extend the right to vote and to political influence much before the twentieth century.

Despite the sentiments popularly attributed to the founding fathers of the United States, the differences across New World societies in who had the right to participate in community decisions were not all that dramatic at a conceptual level as late as the end of the eighteenth century. The British colonies on the mainland, like those elsewhere in the hemisphere, reserved the privilege of voting to white adult men with significant holdings of real estate; inequalities in landholding across colonies as well as in the specified thresholds meant that the same sort of limitation on the franchise implied very different proportions of the population eligible to vote.[8] This practice was rooted in a philosophy that can be traced back at least as far as medieval Britain, in which the right to vote should be reserved to "freeholders," who because of their stake in land had more of a long-term interest in the welfare of the community (as compared to mere "free men") and thus the right to be a decisionmaker and voter.[9] It treated communities as akin to business corporations; given that the colonies were commercial enterprises, it was perhaps an especially natural extension. Landowners were analogous to shareholders and entitled to vote; indeed, nonresidents were frequently permitted to vote where they owned property. Over time, as the colonies developed beyond commercial enterprises and became more diverse socially and economically, the restrictions on suffrage evolved to take account of a more complex society.

It is difficult to identify a single philosophy that guided the articulation or progression of qualifications for suffrage across the British colonies on the mainland. Instead, two general considerations might be said to have framed the political debates, with their relative influences varying over context. One focused on the individual and was concerned with what characteristics gave a person the right to vote; was it the ownership of property, the payment of taxes, residency, or simply being an adult white male? The other general consideration in setting the qualifications was what would

8. Kirk H. Porter, *A History of Suffrage in the United States* (Chicago: University of Chicago Press, 1918); and Chilton Williamson, *American Suffrage: From Property to Democracy 1760–1860* (Princeton, N.J.: Princeton University Press, 1960).

9. See Williamson, *American Suffrage*, for a discussion of precedents, as well as of the range of freehold requirements in the colonies. Long-term leases, extending beyond a lifetime, were sometimes accepted as satisfying such qualifications.

be good for the community or the society. Would it be in the best interests of the society for nonresidents, nonproperty holders, illiterates, criminals, or nonchurch-members to be allowed to vote? Overall, the dominant trend over the colonial period was the movement away from the idea that the right to vote should be based solely on the ownership of land. There was a growing appreciation of how suffrage qualifications specified along this single dimension might exclude otherwise appropriate individuals—especially in urban settings. Over time, colonies began to introduce means of substituting other assets to meet property requirements, and this development ultimately led to the acceptance of qualifications based on the amount of tax payments. However, in no colony does there appear to have been a truly serious challenge to the notion that suffrage should be restricted to property owners.[10]

All thirteen colonies maintained some sort of property qualification for the franchise on the eve of the American Revolution. Georgia, North Carolina, Virginia, New Jersey, New Hampshire, New York, and Rhode Island had minimum real estate requirements, specified in terms of either acreage or value. The remaining six colonies allowed for more flexibility, with the property requirement allowing either landholding, ownership of some other property exceeding a specified minimum, or (in the case of South Carolina) payment of a certain amount of taxes. Given the issues at stake in the conflict between the thirteen colonies and Britain, it should not be surprising that the question of suffrage reform was central to many of the intense debates about the organization of state governments conducted in the aftermath of the Declaration of Independence. Although some states, such as Rhode Is-

---

10. There were often different qualifications for local elections than for colony-wide elections, and Williamson, *American Suffrage*, has suggested that one reason for this was to increase the pool of individuals who could be co-opted to serve as local officials.

land, merely carried over the voting qualifications in place during the colonial era, eight of the thirteen made substantial changes through the constitutions they adopted during the revolutionary era. Most moved in the direction of expanding the franchise somewhat, whether by providing for alternative ways of meeting standards for property holders or by adopting differential requirements for elections to different posts (such as New York's having higher property requirements for the election of state senators and the governor than for the election of members of its assembly). Only Pennsylvania eliminated wealth qualifications (replacing them with a tax-paying requirement).[11] The paucity of data makes it difficult to construct estimates of what the effects of these changes on the size of the legal electorate were, but even those scholars who argue that the legal changes were important seem to believe that their de facto effects were modest.[12]

In general, the major break of doing away with all suffrage qualifications related to property or economic standing more generally was led by new states entering the Union (see table 3.1). Not a single state that entered the Union after the original thirteen had a property requirement for the franchise, and although a few adopted a tax-based qualification, it was only in Louisiana that the restriction

11. Economic-based qualifications for suffrage were not the only way in which the wealthier classes were granted privileged status as regards political standing. In 1787 all thirteen states except Pennsylvania had economic qualifications for holding office. In six of the twelve (Maryland, Massachusetts, New Hampshire, North Carolina, New Jersey, and South Carolina) the property requirements were considerably higher for serving as governor, senator, or representative than they were for voting. See Dudley O. McGovney, *The American Suffrage Medley* (Chicago: University of Chicago Press, 1949), chap. 1.

12. Porter, *A History of Suffrage in the United States*, chaps. 1–2. Williamson, *American Suffrage*, appears to be more impressed with the conceptual import of the legal changes during the revolutionary era than was Porter but is at the same time skeptical about their direct impact. McGovney, *The American Suffrage Medley*, suggests that roughly half of the adult white male population was eligible to vote in 1787.

TABLE 3.1
Economic-Based Qualifications for Suffrage

State	Qualification in 1787 or Year of Entry	Year Economic Qualifications Ended, or Qualif. in 1860
Original Thirteen		
New Hampshire	Tax	1792
Massachusetts	Property	1821 (prop.), tax req. in 1860 [a]
Rhode Island	Property	1842 (prop.), tax req. in 1860 [a]
Connecticut	Property	1818 (prop.), 1845 (tax)
New York	Property	1821 (prop.), 1826 (tax)
New Jersey	Property	1807 (prop.), 1844 (tax)
Pennsylvania	Tax	tax req. in 1860 [a]
Delaware	Property	1792 (prop.), tax req. in 1860 [a]
Maryland	Property	1802
Virginia	Property	1850
North Carolina	Property	1856 (prop.), tax req. in 1860 [a]
South Carolina	Tax	1810 (tax)
Georgia	Property	1789 (prop.), 1798 (tax)
New		
Vermont	none (1791)	
Kentucky	none (1792)	
Tennessee	none (1796)	
Ohio	Tax (1803)	1851 (tax)
Louisiana	Tax (1812)	1845 (tax)
Indiana	none (1816)	
Mississippi	Tax (1817)	1832 (tax)
Illinois	none (1818)	
Maine	none (1819)	
Alabama	none (1819)	
Missouri	none (1820)	

[a] Tax req. in 1860 means that a tax-based qualification for suffrage was still in effect in that year.

SOURCES: Kirk H. Porter, *A History of Suffrage in the United States* (Chicago: University of Chicago Press, 1918); and Chilton Williamson, *American Suffrage: From Property to Democracy, 1760–1860* (Princeton, N.J.: Princeton University Press, 1960).

was binding and endured. Most of the original thirteen (all but Rhode Island, Virginia, and North Carolina) had done away with property qualifications by the middle of the 1820s, but tax-based requirements for suffrage (and for the holding of public office) lingered on in many of them into the middle of the nineteenth century and beyond. Also striking is that, of the states formed of the originally settled areas, it was those that were sparsely settled and on the fringe (Vermont, New Hampshire, and Georgia) that seem to have taken the lead in doing away with all economic-based qualifications for the franchise.

The spirit of the Revolution undoubtedly contributed to the movement for the extension of the franchise, but the systematic pattern of where the changes were made seems significant and has attracted much comment.[13] Why were frontier states ahead of the original states that had long histories? A number of possible explanations have been offered. First, the U.S. Constitution laid out a process for new states to join the Union, which may have favored the adoption of state constitutions with universal white male suffrage. Another distinctive feature of the frontier areas that might have contributed to their having fewer restrictions on the right to vote was that they generally had a scarcity of labor. If the

---

13. Although many observers of that time noted how the new states, and especially those in the West, were more democratic in their suffrage laws and in other respects, Frederick Jackson Turner was perhaps the first major scholar to devote much attention to the question of why. See Turner's *The Rise of the New West, 1819–1929* (New York: Harper and Brothers, 1906) and *The Frontier in American History* (New York: Henry Holt, 1920). Williamson, *American Suffrage,* is skeptical of the notion that the West was unique, however, and has suggested that the prevalence of universal suffrage in the frontier states may have been due to the difficulty of establishing freehold rights in a newly settled area where land titling was imperfect and recent. See Richard P. McCormick, "New Perspectives on Jacksonian Politics," *American Historical Review* 65 (1960): 288–301, for estimates of the proportion of adult white males who voted and for discussion of the variation over time and state in voting participation. He too is uncertain that the western states were all that different from those in the East.

right to participate in the political process was desirable to potential migrants, the new states thus had an economic incentive to adopt liberal suffrage provisions (which in turn might have put pressure on other states to alter their laws to remain competitive). The frontier areas also had probably the greatest degree of equality or homogeneity in the population, and where the amount of property owned at a particular point in time was least indicative of an individual's life course or commitment to his community.[14] These conditions could have made it more difficult to sustain a case for discriminating between otherwise similar individuals on the basis of holding a specified amount of wealth at a single point in time.

The actual attainment of universal white adult male suffrage, that is doing away with all economic-based qualifications for the vote, began with Vermont and Kentucky joining the United States in 1791 and 1792. Perhaps inspired by its neighbor, in 1792 New Hampshire—which resembled a frontier area in many respects— swept away the tax-paying qualification it had in 1784 replaced with a rather high property requirement. Although serving to keep suffrage reform a live issue of political debate, these states did not immediately attract a flood of imitators, especially since both Pennsylvania and South Carolina had in 1790 adopted new state constitutions that maintained, in slightly weakened forms, qualifications that were primarily tax based. During the last decade of the eighteenth century, Tennessee joined the Union with a freehold require-

14. For evidence of the relative equality of populations in frontier states, see Lee Soltow, *Men and Wealth in the United States, 1850–1870* (New Haven: Yale University Press, 1975); William H. Newell, "Inheritance on the Maturing Frontier: Butler County, Ohio, 1803–1865," in Stanley L. Engerman and Robert E. Gallman, eds., *Long-Term Factors in American Economic Growth* (Chicago: University of Chicago Press, 1986); and J. R. Kearl and Clayne Pope, "Choices, Rents, and Luck: Economic Mobility of Nineteenth-Century Utah Households," in Stanley L. Engerman and Robert E. Gallman, eds., *Long-Term Factors in American Economic Growth* (Chicago: University of Chicago Press).

ment (but one that was waived for those who had been resident in a county for six months) for suffrage, and Delaware and Georgia revised their laws to set the payment of a state or county tax, or of any assessed taxes, as the test.[15]

The suffrage issue was of course only one of a number of important issues that divided the population, and the political battles, if not alignments, were somewhat different in each state—often not along party lines. In general, however, in the older colonies elites were slower to embrace the changes, the political conflict was greatest (the salient examples include Massachusetts and New York), and economic-based restrictions on the franchise were much slower to disappear. Among new entrants to the Union, no state outside the original thirteen ever had a meaningful property requirement for the suffrage. After Tennessee, the next state to join the Union was Ohio, in 1803, which required that its voters pay a county tax or else work out a tax on the public highway. Louisiana became a state in 1812, with a landholding alternative to a relatively stringent tax qualification; anyone who had purchased land from the U.S. government had the right to vote, as long as he was a white male who had resided in the county in question for a year. The only significant deviation from the pattern among new states, it failed to follow the examples of its southern neighbors like Georgia , Maryland, and South Carolina, which had formally or effectively done away with economic-based requirements and allowed white adult males to qualify for suffrage by length of residency in 1798, 1802, and 1810, respectively.[16]

15. Porter, *A History of Suffrage in the United States*; Williamson, *American Suffrage*; and McCormick, "New Perspectives on Jacksonian Politics."

16. These changes in the state constitutions to extend the suffrage (if not lower the very high wealth requirements for holding office) were highly controversial in both states, with the alignments in favor and in opposition not corresponding all that strongly with political parties. In Maryland, the change is not thought to have had a major impact on the size of the electorate, largely because of limited enforce-

Louisiana notwithstanding, the innovations in suffrage laws over the first two decades of the United States signify a critical juncture. The use of wealth as a basis for distinguishing who should vote was clearly becoming less viable, and the ultimate fate of such qualifications was becoming clear.[17] This did not mean, however, that there was opposition to all restrictions on who could vote. The relatively homogeneous white males might believe that differentiation on the basis of wealth was unfair, unreasonable, or inconsistent with basic rights, especially where wealth was relatively equally distributed and there was substantial social mobility, but they could support the exclusion of groups of the population that were obviously distinctive and arguably unsuitable for participating in community decisions: blacks, the mentally ill, those with criminal records, and those who had not long been resident in the county or state. When there were wealth-based restrictions, there had been no real need for provisions that dealt specifically with these classes, but as states eliminated or weakened the economic qualifications, there was increasing emphasis on introducing or tightening qualifications that would keep them out of the electorate. Indeed, all the suffrage reforms affecting the composition of the electorate were

---

ment of the economic qualification and because depreciation of the state paper money had eroded the import of the threshold estate value. Some other reforms dealing with the conduct of elections, such as the introduction of balloting (as opposed to voice votes) and the expansion of the number of polling places, were also introduced at about the same time. In South Carolina, the movement for suffrage reform coincided with concern about the possibility of war with Britain and seems to have benefited somewhat from the view that those who bore arms in the militia should be able to vote. See Williamson, *American Suffrage*, chap. 8.

17. Mississippi, in 1817, was the last state to enter the Union without universal adult white male suffrage, and from then on the maintenance of economic-based restrictions was largely a holding action. Many of the original thirteen states replaced wealth qualifications with tax-based requirements (which endured in some states for a very long period), but it is not clear how binding they were. Of course, the use of poll taxes expanded greatly in the late nineteenth and early twentieth centuries as a way of obstructing blacks and immigrants from voting.

generally adopted at the same time. Despite virtually all the new states beyond the original thirteen entering the Union with weak or no economic requirements for the franchise, Kentucky (and it only for a brief period) and Vermont were the only ones that allowed blacks to vote. The list of those that never allowed blacks to vote before the Fourteenth Amendment include California, Colorado, Illinois, Indiana, Iowa, Kansas, Michigan, Minnesota, Missouri, Nebraska, Nevada, Ohio, Oregon, Utah, Wisconsin, as well as all the southern states. Moreover, at the same time that Delaware, Maryland, Connecticut, New Jersey, and Pennsylvania eased their economic qualifications, each altered their constitution to exclude blacks. On the eve of the Civil War, the only states that extended the franchise to blacks were those in New England, where those of African descent were exceptionally rare, and New York (where a property requirement of $250 was applied to blacks but not to whites).[18]

Indiana, Illinois, and Missouri were brought into the nation between 1815 and 1820, and none had any suffrage qualification related to wealth or to tax payments. There was little support within the relatively homogeneous populations of the western states for drawing a line to distinguish the franchised from the disenfranchised among white adult males; indeed, a modest proposal to require a tax payment was voted down resoundingly in the Missouri constitutional convention of 1820. Indeed, after Ohio in 1803, no northern state admitted to the Union came in with a property or taxpaying qualification (and no southern state, after Mississippi in 1817). Residency requirements, strictures on race, gender, and age, as well as disqualifications for infamous crimes were the only constraints on suffrage imposed in the more newly settled areas. Else-

18. See the discussion in Porter, *A History of Suffrage in the United States,* chaps. 2–4; and Kenneth M. Stampp, *America in 1857: A Nation on the Brink* (New York: Oxford University Press, 1990), p. 134.

where, the significance of property was definitely on the wane but remained an issue. Maine, once part of Massachusetts, joined the United States in 1819, and its constitutional convention issued a public statement describing its stand on the question: "Pecuniary qualifications have been productive of little benefit; sometimes of injustice. They are too often relaxed or strained to suit the purposes of the day. The convention has therefore extended the right of suffrage, so that no person is disqualified for want of property unless he be a pauper."[19] Of the two new southern states established during these years, Alabama made no reference to property in its laws, but Mississippi did adopt a requirement (that was abandoned in 1832) of either a tax payment or service in the state militia. Both states devoted considerable attention to specifying which classes of the population could vote, and which—mostly various classes of criminals—could not. Lines continued to be drawn, but the population was increasingly skeptical of positioning them on the basis of pecuniary factors.

Property- or tax-based qualifications were most strongly entrenched in the original thirteen states, and the most dramatic political battles took place at a series of prominent constitutional conventions held in those states during late in the second decade of the 1800s and the 1820s. For example, although the Committee on Elective Franchise to the New York State convention had recommended in 1821 to abolish all property distinctions and require only virtue and morality of voters, opponents of universal suffrage put up a spirited defense. After lengthy discussion, and a strong vote against an explicit property qualification, a compromise plan that offered a wide set of alternatives was enacted: a voter must have paid a state or county tax, have performed military service, have worked on a public highway, or have lived three years in the state (instead of the ordinary one-year requirement); in 1826, these qual-

19. Porter, *A History of Suffrage in the United States*, pp. 50–51.

ifications were dispensed with in favor of universal white adult male suffrage for residents.[20] Another heated debate took place at the Massachusetts convention of 1820, where notables such as John Adams, Daniel Webster, and Joseph Storey warned of the consequences of extending the franchise. Although their eloquence was not sufficient to save a property qualification, the new constitution did include a requirement that either a county or state tax had been paid.

These vigorous political struggles were repeated in virtually all the states that retained property- or tax-based qualification, with a gradual winnowing down of the restrictions—often to the point of a token tax payment of a dollar or two. Because of the progressive erosion of the requirements even within those states that maintained them, our limited knowledge about patterns of wealth holding and tax payments, and shifts in the regional distribution of the population, it is difficult at present to construct precise estimates of how the eligible pool of voters changed over time. Comparisons of the number of votes cast with the adult white male population, however, indicate that a high rate of voter participation was realized early in the nineteenth century (see table 3.2). These figures, which reproduce estimates prepared by McCormick, suggest that by 1820 more than half of adult white males were casting votes in nearly all states—with the prominent exceptions of those that still retained property requirements: Virginia, Rhode Island, and New York as well as Louisiana (which had an unusually stringent tax requirement) and Ohio (also a tax requirement). McCormick's estimates are puzzling in that they reveal much higher voting rates in early nonpresidential elections than in the presidential election, in which Andrew Jackson was a candidate, but he argues that local issues

20. See the discussions in Porter, *A History of Suffrage in the United States;* Williamson, *American Suffrage;* and Marchette Chute, *The First Liberty: A History of the Right to Vote in America, 1619–1850* (New York: Dutton, 1969).

TABLE 3.2
Adult White Males Voting in Elections (in percentage)

State	Year	Before 1824	PRESIDENTIAL ELECTIONS 1824	1828	1832	1836	1840	1844
Maine	1812	62.0%	18.9%	42.7%	66.2%	37.4%	82.2%	67.5%
New Hampshire	1814	80.8	16.8	76.5	74.2	38.2	86.4	65.6
Vermont	1812	79.9	—	55.8	50.0	52.5	74.0	65.7
Massachusetts	1812	67.4	29.1	25.7	39.3	45.1	66.4	59.3
Rhode Island	*1812*	*49.4*	*12.4*	*18.0*	*22.4*	*24.1*	*33.2*	*39.8*
Connecticut	1819	54.5	14.9	27.1	45.9	52.3	75.7	76.1
New York	1810	*41.5*	—	70.4	72.1	60.2	77.7	73.6
New Jersey	1808	71.8	31.1	70.9	60.9	69.3	80.4	81.6
Pennsylvania	1808	71.5	19.6	56.6	52.7	53.1	77.4	75.5
Delaware	1804	81.9	—	—	67.0	69.4	82.8	85.0
Maryland	1820	69.0	53.7	76.2	55.6	67.5	84.6	80.3
Virginia	*1800*	*25.9*	*11.5*	*27.6*	*30.8*	*35.1*	*54.6*	*54.5*
North Carolina	—	—	42.2	56.8	31.7	52.9	83.1	79.1
Georgia	1812	62.3	—	35.9	33.0	64.9	88.9	94.0
Kentucky	1820	74.4	25.3	70.7	73.9	61.1	74.3	80.3
Tennessee	1817	80.0	26.8	49.8	28.8	55.2	89.6	89.6
Louisiana	*1812*	*34.2*	—	*36.3*	*24.4*	*19.2*	*39.4*	*44.7*
Alabama	1819	96.7	52.1	53.6	33.3	65.0	89.8	82.7
Mississippi	1823	79.8	41.6	56.6	32.8	62.8	88.2	89.7
Ohio	1822	46.5	34.8	75.8	73.8	75.5	84.5	83.6
Indiana	1822	52.4	37.5	68.3	61.8	70.1	86.0	84.9
Illinois	1822	55.8	24.2	51.9	45.6	43.7	85.9	76.3
Missouri	1820	71.9	20.1	54.3	40.8	35.6	74.0	74.7
AVERAGE			26.5	56.3	54.9	55.2	78.0	74.9

NOTE: The elections that were conducted under a property-based requirement for the franchise appear in italics. Although North Carolina had a property qualification in voting for certain state posts, there appears to have been none in the presidential elections. The Louisiana figures also appear in italics because McCormick characterized its tax-based qualification as unusually stringent. The estimates of the highest proportions of adult males voting before 1824 were prepared by McCormick because of his desire to highlight how participation in the elections during the Jacksonian period was not exceptionally high. As McCormick recognized, it is potentially misleading to use the highest figure before 1824 as the basis for comparison; the examination of the record over time is complicated by the changes that were made in the methods of electing governors and presidential electors, but he reports that the average voter participation before 1824 was obviously higher (than in the three Jackson elections) in Alabama, Connecticut, Massachusetts, Mississippi, New Hampshire, Pennsylvania, Rhode Island, Tennessee, and Vermont.

SOURCES: Richard P. McCormick, "New Perspectives on Jacksonian Politics," *American Historical Review* 65 (1960): 288–301.

were much more important during this era and that presidential races were not generally seriously contested at the state level. The traditional notion that it was Jackson and his Democratic Party that brought forth mass voting participation does not seem consistent with this evidence, but it does support the notion that broad participation coincided with the adoption of laws that extended suffrage. As is reflected in the consistently lower voting rates of Rhode Island and Virginia (the two states that maintained property restrictions through 1840), part of the higher rates of the era were due to the changes in the laws governing suffrage. But the figures also bolster the view that a broad mass of the population was interested in exercising political influence and that this sentiment contributed to the way in which the suffrage institutions evolved. Given the interest in voting that McCormick's figures suggest, it may have been difficult for legislators or participants in constitutional conventions not to extend suffrage.

By 1840, there were only three states that retained a property qualification: North Carolina (for some statewide offices only), Rhode Island, and Virginia, and North Carolina in 1856 was the last state to end the practice. Taxpaying qualifications were also gone in all but a few states by the Civil War, but they did survive into the twentieth century in Pennsylvania and Rhode Island.[21] Poll taxes were revived during the 1890s and the first decade of the twentieth century, along with the introduction of literacy tests, as a number of southern states revised their constitutions or enacted new laws to sharply restrict voting by blacks.[22] This effort was successful, and the experience of blacks in the South—when they were flagrantly denied equal access to public services during their period of disfran-

21. Porter, *A History of Suffrage in the United States*, chap. 4.
22. The institution of literacy tests was not confined to the South. Eighteen states, seven southern and eleven nonsouthern, introduced literacy requirements between 1890 and 1926. They were directed primarily at blacks and immigrants.

chisement even as a free people—dramatizes how important the right to vote can be.[23] As obvious and consequential as this episode of systematic action to deny a salient social group a significant political voice was, what stands out from the U.S. record is how relatively rare such measures were—at least as judged by the proportion of the population affected (compared with virtually all of the other societies in the hemisphere). Women, blacks, and youth were the principal sufferers of restrictions on the franchise. The relative paucity of binding requirements on white male adult voters does not appear to have been due to philosophical positions that everyone or even every man had an innate right to vote. Qualifications based on race, residency, as well as on criminal record and mental health, were too commonplace for the notion of voting being a basic right. On the contrary, the pattern by which such qualifications were introduced and stiffened as property and tax-based standards were relaxed or abandoned suggests that the requirements for the franchise were being set through a process that accepted the drawing of lines but would change or vary them depending on circumstances. As to what circumstances favored universal white manhood suffrage, perhaps the most telling is that the western or frontier states, together with highly rural northern ones, were the first movers.

The weakening and ultimate removal of wealth-based restrictions on the franchise seems likely to have been an important contributor, together with the spread of more secrecy in balloting and other reforms in the conduct of elections, to a substantial increase in the fraction of the population voting in U.S. elections. But it was only one. Although McCormick's figures suggest a reinterpretation may be in order, the age of Andrew Jackson is frequently depicted as one of broad advance in political participation, and the propor-

23. See J. Morgan Kousser, *The Shaping of Southern Politics: Suffrage Restrictions and the Establishment of the One-Party South, 1880–1910* (New Haven: Yale University Press, 1974).

tion of adult white males voting in presidential elections did rise sharply between 1824 and 1840. Whatever the distribution of responsibility, the United States had among the highest, if not the highest, proportion of the population voting in the world by the middle of the nineteenth century. None of the Latin American countries would equal this rate of suffrage for another seventy-five years. Indeed, throughout the hemisphere, only Canada, where similar movements for the extension of the franchise with similar outcomes lagged those in the United States by nearly a half-century, was much of a rival in political participation.

In the middle of the nineteenth century the United States had perhaps one and a half times the rate of population voting as did Canada, and eight or more times the rate as elsewhere in the hemisphere (see table 3.3). Given that most of these societies were at least nominal democracies, it is reasonable to ask where this extraordinary gap in the rate of the fundamental political participation that is voting came from. The chief issue, of course, is whether the gap in the proportions of the population voting was due to differences in the numbers eligible to vote under law or to some other disparity in conditions, and if it was attributable to differences in qualifications for the suffrage, what accounted for the contrast in the laws? Even a cursory examination of the requirements for voting in the Americas is sufficient to demonstrate that they were much more restrictive than in the United States or Canada and thus would be expected to have yielded much lower rates of voting. Not only were qualifications based on wealth or income common, but the requirement of literacy came to be virtually universal as well. These strictures, which were generally set forth as qualifications for being a citizen, effectively barred the great majority of wage earners, whether urban or rural, and of Native Americans from voting. In such a legal environment, with extremely low literacy rates (perpetuated by lack of support for public schools until late in the nineteenth or early twentieth centuries), and unequal distributions of

TABLE 3.3

Laws Governing the Franchise and the Extent of Voting
in Selected American Countries, 1840–1940

Country	Years	Lack of Secrecy in Balloting	Wealth Requirement	Literacy Requirement	Proportion of the Population Voting
	1840–1880				
Chile	1869	No	Yes	Yes	1.6%
	1878	No	No	No [a]	—
Costa Rica	1890	Yes	Yes	Yes	—
Ecuador	1848	Yes	Yes	Yes	0.0
	1856	Yes	Yes	Yes	0.1
Mexico	1840	Yes	Yes	Yes	—
Peru	1875	Yes	Yes	Yes	—
Uruguay	1840	Yes	Yes	Yes	—
	1880	Yes	Yes	Yes	—
Venezuela	1840	Yes	Yes	Yes	—
	1880	Yes	Yes	Yes	—
Canada	1867	Yes	Yes	No	7.7
	1878	No	Yes	No	12.9
United States	1850 [b]	No	No	No	12.9
	1880	No	No	No	18.3
	1881–1920				
Argentina	1896	Yes	Yes	Yes	1.8% [c]
	1916	No	No	No	9.0
Brazil	1894	Yes	Yes	Yes	2.2
	1914	Yes	Yes	Yes	2.4
Chile	1881	No	No	No	3.1
	1920	No	No	Yes	4.4
Colombia	1918 [d]	No	No	No	6.9
Costa Rica	1912	Yes	Yes	Yes	—
	1919	Yes	No	No	10.6
Ecuador	1888	No	Yes	Yes	2.8
	1894	No	No	Yes	3.3
Mexico	1920	No	No	No	8.6
Peru	1920	Yes	Yes	Yes	—
Uruguay	1900	Yes	Yes	Yes	—
	1920	No	No	No	13.8
Venezuela	1920	Yes	Yes	Yes	—
Canada	1911	No	No	No	18.1
	1917	No	No	No	20.5
United States	1900	No	No	Yes [e]	18.4
	1920	No	No	Yes	25.1

TABLE 3.3
(continued)

Country	Years	Lack of Secrecy in Balloting	Wealth Requirement	Literacy Requirement	Proportion of the Population Voting
	1921–1940				
Argentina	1928	No	No	No	12.8%
	1937	No	No	No	15.0
Bolivia	1951	—	Yes	Yes	4.1
Brazil	1930	Yes	Yes	Yes	5.7
Colombia	1930	No	No	No	11.1
	1936	No	No	No	5.9
Chile	1920	No	No	Yes	4.4
	1931	No	No	Yes	6.5
	1938	No	No	Yes	9.4
Costa Rica	1940	No	No	No	17.6
Ecuador	1940	No	No	Yes	3.3
Mexico	1940	No	No	No	11.8
Peru	1940	No	No	Yes	—
Uruguay	1940	No	No	No	19.7
Venezuela	1940	No	Yes	Yes	—
Canada	1940	No	No	No	41.1
United States	1940	No	No	Yes	37.8

[a] After eliminating wealth and education requirements in 1878, Chile instituted a literacy requirement in 1885, which seems to have been responsible for a sharp decline in the proportion of the population that was registered to vote.

[b] Three states, Connecticut, Louisiana, and New Jersey, still maintained wealth requirements in 1840, but eliminated them soon afterward. All states except Illinois and Virginia had implemented the secret ballot by the end of the 1840s.

[c] This figure is for the city of Buenos Aires and likely overstates the proportion that voted at the national level.

[d] The information on restrictions refers to national laws. The 1863 constitution empowered provincial state governments to regulate electoral affairs. Afterward, elections became restricted (in terms of the franchise for adult males) and indirect in some states. It was not until 1948 that a national law established universal adult male suffrage throughout the country. This pattern was followed in other Latin American countries, as it was in the United States and Canada to a lesser extent.

[e] Eighteen states, seven southern and eleven nonsouthern, introduced literacy requirements between 1890 and 1926. These restrictions were directed primarily at African Americans and immigrants.

SOURCE: Stanley L. Engerman, Stephen Haber, and Kenneth L. Sokoloff, "Inequality, Institutions, and Differential Paths of Growth among New World Economies," in Claude Menard, ed., *Institutions, Contracts, and Organizations* (Cheltenham, U.K.: Edward Elgar, 2000).

land and wealth more generally, it is not surprising that the proportion of the populations voting was no higher than 1 or 2 percent until late in the nineteenth century. Even the most progressive of the Latin American societies were seventy-five years behind the United States in voter participation.

The exclusion of nonproperty-owners from the standing to vote, and from other rights of citizens, by the independent Latin American nations continued the tradition inherited from the political institutions and policies put in place during the colonial period by Spanish authorities. Although the major figures in the Spanish colonial administrations were appointed by the Crown, or by its colonial representatives, municipal councils (*cabildos*) with elected members were allowed some significant political jurisdiction (including authority to levy taxes) to provide local public services. Each cabildo typically—though not always— originated with a set of appointed council members drawn from prominent citizens (*vecinos*) of the municipality (*pueblo*) but was later extended through elections of members. Participation in such elections (and frequently membership on the council as well as the holding of other offices) was generally restricted to substantial landowners (and sometimes even confined to the council members themselves).[24] In restricting the right to vote to an elite propertied class, the regulation of suffrage in the Spanish colonies resembled that in the English colonies but was much more restrictive with respect to the proportion of the population that had voting rights. Given this history, it should perhaps not be surprising that after they gained independence, these societies—again like their counterparts to the north—continued to

24. Stanley J. Stein and Barbara H. Stein, *The Colonial Heritage of Latin America* (Oxford: Oxford Press, 1970); Lockhart and Schwartz, *Early Latin America*; and Constantino Bayle, *Los Cabildos Seculares en la América Española* (Madrid: Sapientia, 1952).

restrict the franchise on the basis of characteristics directly related to wealth.

Like the United States, however, the nature and centrality of the suffrage qualifications based on wealth-related variables changed. Although systematic information allowing for quantitative assessment of patterns has not yet been retrieved, restrictions that had often been specified in terms of ownership of land during the colonial period were made more flexible after independence. In early constitutions, and increasingly over time, qualifications for voting were revised to encompass those who owned different types of property (other than land), satisfied an income threshold, or even had a certain social standing or professional occupation. Scholars of Latin America have often attributed these sorts of changes in post-independence political institutions to the interests of the *criollo* elite—who had been at the forefront of the independence movement and whose power was very much enhanced by gaining independence from Spain. It is suggested that the criollo were much broader in composition than, if not distinct from, the major landowning families and that they accordingly favored reducing the importance of land relative to other gauges of economic and social standing.[25] An alternative measure of status that came to be extensively employed in the laws was the ability to read and write—a capacity that was rare in these societies, especially among Native Americans. In time the literacy test evolved to become the dominant standard; for example, in its 1859 constitution, Chile recognized literate males as having sufficient income to meet the qualification for the franchise.

Indeed, the introduction and growing emphasis on a literacy requirement was the major change that occurred after independence in the laws governing the franchise. This development is re-

25. Stein and Stein, *The Colonial Heritage of Latin America,* chap. 6.

markable not only for spreading rapidly throughout Latin America but also for being rather novel for the New World. Whereas a literacy qualification was not used in the United States until the 1890s, when the black population was targeted for disfranchisement in the South (and perhaps blacks and immigrants in the North), virtually all Latin American countries included a literacy requirement for citizenship (encompassing the right to vote) in their first constitution or soon afterward. For example, Bolivia advanced a literacy restriction in its 1826 constitution that was maintained beyond the 1945 constitution; Costa Rica had one in its first constitution as an independent state (1844) but eliminated it in 1913; Chile had a literacy requirement between 1833 and 1874 and then from 1885 through 1970; Ecuador abandoned its property requirements for voters in its 1861 constitution but replaced them with a literacy requirement (which endured until 1978); El Salvador had a literacy restriction in its first constitution as an independent state (1864) but seems to have eliminated it in 1945; Guatemala had a literacy restriction in its first full constitution (1879) and maintained it through its 1945 constitution (when illiterates were given the right to a public vote—illiterates with a profession were given the right to vote in 1935); Mexico had a literacy qualification in its 1835 constitution but did away with it in the 1857 constitution (which also nationalized church property and set off a civil war); Peru had a literacy qualification in its 1826 constitution that was largely maintained through 1979 (there have been more than twenty constitutions, and a few of them prior to 1979 relaxed the qualification albeit briefly); and Uruguay had a literacy requirement from the 1830 constitution until the 1918 constitution. Brazil, despite a different national heritage, also had property-based restrictions after independence, but replaced them with a literacy qualification in 1891; this restriction endured until 1988. Overall, the only major Latin American countries that did not have had literacy requirements at the national level were Argentina and Colombia. In both of these cases, states or provinces were allowed considerable latitude in regulating elections and voting, and it seems that some did impose literacy qualifications.[26]

To an even greater extent than in the United States, the requirements for suffrage seem to have made a difference in the rates of political participation across Latin America. The countries with the most progressive suffrage laws (Argentina, Costa Rica, and Uruguay, which led in extending the franchise early in the twentieth century) had markedly higher rates of the population voting (see table 3.3). That the literacy restrictions could have had such a great impact on participation in elections is evident from the exceptionally low literacy rates in Latin America (see table 3.4), and indeed nearly everywhere in the hemisphere, except the United States and Canada, until the twentieth century. Within countries, even the short-term responses to laws extending suffrage were significant in terms of increasing the proportions of the population voting. For example, after the literacy requirement in Chile was removed by the 1874 constitution (an action reversed in 1885), the proportion of voters in the population more than tripled within a few years. In Argentina, the 1912 reform that introduced the so-called Australian ballot, with secrecy and standardized public ballots, as well as universal and compulsory suffrage for men over eighteen, led to a rapid and dramatic increase in political participation, as "voting increased threefold or fourfold in the parliamentary elections of 1912, 1913, and 1914, and rose still further in the presidential elections of 1916."[27] Indeed, the change in the law is generally credited with being responsible for an historic defeat of the long-dominant National Autonomist party (PAN) and the election of the presidential

26. See the discussion of the evolution of constitutions within the various countries in Russell H. Fitzgibbon, *The Constitutions of the Americas* (Chicago: University of Chicago Press, 1948).

27. Leslie Bethell, ed., *Argentina Since Independence* (Cambridge, England: Cambridge University Press, 1993), p. 109.

TABLE 3.4
Literacy Rates in the Americas, 1850–1950

Country	Year	Ages	Rate
Argentina	1869	6+	23.8%
	1895	6+	45.6
	1900	10+	52.0
	1925	10+	73.0
Barbados	1946	10+	92.7
Bolivia	1900	10+	17.0
Brazil	1872	7+	15.8
	1890	7+	14.8
	1900	7+	25.6
	1920	10+	30.0
	1939	10+	57.0
British Honduras	1911	10+	59.6
(Belize)	1931	10+	71.8
Chile	1865	7+	18.0
	1875	7+	25.7
	1885	7+	30.3
	1900	10+	43.0
	1925	10+	66.0
	1945	10+	76.0
Colombia	1918	15+	32.0
	1938	15+	56.0
	1951	15+	62.0
Costa Rica	1892	7+	23.6
	1900	10+	33.0
	1925	10+	64.0
Cuba	1861	7+	23.8
			(38.5,5.3) [a]
	1899	10+	40.5
	1925	10+	67.0
	1946	10+	77.9
Guatemala	1893	7+	11.3
	1925	10+	15.0
	1945	10+	20.0
Honduras	1887	7+	15.2
	1925	10+	29.0

TABLE 3.4
(continued)

Country	Year	Ages	Rate
Jamaica	1871	5+	16.3
	1891	5+	32.0
	1911	5+	47.2
	1943	5+	67.9
	1943	10+	76.1
Mexico	1900	10+	22.2
	1925	10+	36.0
	1946	10+	48.4
Paraguay	1886	7+	19.3
	1900	10+	30.0
Peru	1925	10+	38.0
Puerto Rico	1860	7+	11.8
			(19.8,3.1) [a]
Uruguay	1900	10+	54.0
	1925	10+	70.0
Venezuela	1925	10+	34.0
Canada	1861	All	82.5
English-majority counties	1861	All	93.0
French-majority counties	1861	All	81.2
United States			
North whites	1860	10+	96.9
South whites	1860	10+	56.4
All	1870	10+	80.0
			(88.5,21.1) [a]
	1890	10+	86.7
			(92.3,43.2) [a]
	1910	10+	92.3
			(95.0,69.5) [a]

[a] The figures for whites and nonwhites are reported respectively within parentheses.

SOURCE: Stanley L. Engerman, Stephen Haber, and Kenneth L. Sokoloff, "Inequality, Institutions, and Differential Paths of Growth among New World Economies," in Claude Menard, ed., *Institutions, Contracts, and Organizations* (Cheltenham, U.K.: Edward Elgar, 2000).

candidate of the Radical Civic Union, the principal opposition. Such evidence that the extent of the franchise mattered both quantitatively and qualitatively is consistent with the observation that intense political debates normally surrounded changes in the suffrage laws in all these countries.

The record of suffrage in the Americas highlights a series of fundamental questions about the evolution of political institutions. What factors account for the systematic variation across the societies of the New World in the tightness of the restrictions on who was eligible to vote, and in the fraction of the population that voted? What factors accounted for the variation in form of the restrictions over place and time, and did they matter? What were the effects of these restrictions within the respective societies?

These important issues, and the relevance of the evidence reviewed here, deserve further study. Nevertheless, a few observations seem warranted at this point. First, as regards the existence and sources of systematic variation in the extent of suffrage, there seems no doubt that although there were some striking parallels across the New World societies in their suffrage institutions, especially during the colonial period, some clear patterns in the differences between them are evident. In particular, states or countries with greater homogeneity or equality (broadly defined) among the population tended to extend the franchise earlier and more broadly—contributing to the evolution, or persistence, of a more equal distribution of political influence. This general regularity is suggested not only by the contrast between the English colonies on the North American mainland and the Spanish colonies throughout the New World but also by the variation in experience across the states/societies with the same national heritage. It was, for example, the western or frontier states within the United States, where labor was relatively scarce and both human and nonhuman capital relatively equally distributed, that took the lead in doing away with wealth- or income-based qualifications for the franchise and establishing universal white male suffrage. Moreover (if perhaps trivially), the binding qualifications that were retained for males—based on race—applied to a smaller fraction of the population in those states where the population was more homogeneous.

Why the states in the United States at first moved from economic-based to race-based qualifications for suffrage, instead of the Latin American pattern of going from economic-based to literacy-based qualifications, is a fascinating and important question. Although eliminating economic-based qualifications, such as land, other forms of wealth, income, or taxes paid, extended the franchise to some groups, the adoption of the new set of qualifications was clearly intended by those who played a role in designing the new laws to disfranchise other groups. It does not seem obvious that the elites in the North American states/societies were more ideologically committed to broad suffrage than their counterparts to the south. Both acted to exclude a segment of the male population that was perceived to be very distinct. In the United States, this distinct class composed a smaller proportion of the population than the distinct classes of most of the Latin American societies did. The situation in the United States was perhaps also different from Latin America in that, until the Fourteenth Amendment, race could be explicitly specified as a qualification for suffrage. In Latin America, for whatever reason—perhaps cultural, perhaps due to the greater continuity in the racial distribution of the population—explicit use of race or ethnic background as a requirement for suffrage does not seem to have been feasible. The Latin American pattern (excepting Argentina) of employing literacy as a requirement for suffrage (and citizenship) not only excluded large fractions of the respective populations from voting but may also have had the pathological effect of discouraging elites from investing in the establishment of an extensive system of public schools.

At least at the national level, the hypothesis that societies with greater homogeneity or equality tended to adopt suffrage institutions that provided broader suffrage or a more equal distribution of political influence seems to be consistent with a preliminary examination of the historical record in Latin America. Those countries that are thought to have had more homogeneous populations, as well as greater equality, such as Argentina, Uruguay, and Costa Rica, were the first to implement suffrage institutions associated with more extensive access to and use of the franchise. Although this pattern is consistent with the hypothesis, the limited information available means that this is but a weak test. More evidence needs to be retrieved, and it would be especially interesting to identify the variation in suffrage institutions across the provinces/states of Argentina, Colombia, and other countries that—like the United States—allowed such jurisdictions to set the qualifications for voting.

Finally, there is the question of whether the patterns in how the suffrage institutions evolved made a difference for long-run patterns of economic development. In theory they should, if governments in nominal democracies are influenced by voters, and if the voters have systematic preferences about the economic policies that are on the agenda. A vast literature suggests that governments are responsive to the preferences of their respective electorates; the salient case of what happened to blacks in the U.S. South when they were effectively disfranchised by the diffusion of literacy tests and poll taxes between 1890 and 1910 (to cite a familiar and well-accepted example) seems highly relevant to the contexts considered here.[28] Moreover, Stanley Engerman, Elisa Mariscal, and I have argued elsewhere that the variation in the extent of the franchise across the societies of the New World was associated with invest-

---

28. Powerful examples of how changes in the composition of the electorate can lead to changes in government policy are detailed in Kousser, *The Shaping of Southern Politics*; and John R. Lott Jr. and Lawrence W. Kenny, "Did Women's Suffrage Change the Size and Scope of Government?" *Journal of Political Economy* 10 (1999): 1163–1198.

ment in public schooling and literacy attainment—even after controlling for per capita income.[29] This association, if it reflects a more general relation between the distribution of political influence and public policies, would suggest that the evolution of suffrage institutions might encompass a mechanism by which relative differences across societies in the extent of inequality generally might persist over time, and might—in the case of New World economies—help understand differences in rates of economic growth over the long run.

29. Stanley L. Engerman, Elisa V. Mariscal, and Kenneth L. Sokoloff, "The Persistence of Inequality in the Americas: Schooling and Suffrage, 1800–1945," working paper, University of California, Los Angeles, 1999.

Party and Faction in the
Imperial Brazilian Parliament

Historians of Brazil have long stressed the cronyist nature of nine-teenth-century politics and have enjoyed considerable success in documenting it as well.[1] Patronage, in the form of using resources of the central government to award positions and pork as a private payoff for political support, is the most salient example of cronyist impulse in imperial Brazil.[2] Nonetheless, there has been relatively little work devoted to identifying the interaction between the cronyism on the one hand and formal political institutions on the other. The politics of patronage necessarily entailed tax and expenditure policies on the part of Brazil's government that held both

1. This paper was written while I was a national fellow at the Hoover Institution, Stanford University. It draws from research generously supported by a U.S. Department of Education Fulbright-Hays Faculty Research Abroad Grant, International Studies and Overseas Programs at the University of California at Los Angeles, and the Social Science History Institute at Stanford University. Earlier versions benefited from conversations with José Murilo de Carvalho, Stephen Haber, Nolan McCarty, Jean-Laurent Rosenthal, and Barry Weingast and from the comments of participants at the Conference on Institutions and Markets in Historical Perspective, Stanford; the Fourth International Conference of the Americas, Puebla, Mexico; and the all–University of California Latin American history meeting. All errors are mine.
    2. A richly detailed study of the networks of political patronage is provided by Richard Graham, *Patronage and Politics in Nineteenth-Century Brazil* (Stanford: Stanford University Press, 1990).

allocative and distributive consequences. These were of special significance in Brazil, given both the highly centralized division of authority that characterized its polity and its poor record of economic growth in this period.[3] Since such policies were elaborated within a well-defined set of political institutions and organizations to include party-based cabinets and party affiliations on the floor of the Parliament, they were subject to the influence of Brazilian political organization. This chapter reassesses the role of political parties in imperial Brazil by examining voting patterns on the floor of the lower house of Parliament between 1881 and 1884. The main result is that most voting by deputies in the chamber divided along party lines, as deputies hewed to partisan positions. On those occasions when factions split off from parties, constituent interests indeed overrode party positions to pull deputies away from party objectives. But the evidence here shows that factionalization around constituent interests was of second-order importance in policymaking. In light of the findings of this chapter, the historiography understates the significance of political parties in transforming cronyism into particular economic policies. Although it is not possible to attribute all the pattern of party-based voting to the influence of party organizations, parties did command considerable electoral resources that were valued by deputies. Most important, the economic consequences of strong party organizations in the Chamber of Deputies were positive. By acting in concert, party partisans adopted mea-

3. For a detailed discussion of the structure of the Brazilian state under the 1824 constitution, see Marquês de José Antônio Pimenta Bueno Sao Vicente, *Direito Publico Brazileiro E Analyse Da Constituição Do Imperio* (Rio de Janeiro: Typ. de J. Villeneuve, 1857). On the economic consequences of centralized policymaking in general, see Robert P. Inman and Daniel L. Rubinfeld, "The Political Economy of Federalism," in Dennis C. Mueller, ed., *Perspectives on Public Choice* (Cambridge, England: Cambridge University Press, 1997). The average rate of growth in per capita GDP in Brazil was barely positive over the course of the nineteenth century. For estimates and a study of the economic factors at work, see Nathaniel H. Leff, *Underdevelopment and Development in Brazil* (London: Allen & Unwin, 1982).

sures that were less distortionary than would have been attained by independently pursuing the politics of the pork barrel. Although the magnitude of this effect cannot be stated with any precision, its direction is clear: partisan politics impelled policies that helped off-set the negative economic consequences of Brazil's highly central-ized division of authority.

This chapter examines three questions about the Brazilian Chamber of Deputies, using the early 1880s as a case study. Did Brazilian parties exhibit different voting patterns on the floor of the Chamber of Deputies? Did members of each party cohere, voting with their partisan colleagues? What influence did party affiliation play in explaining the voting records of each individual deputy rel-ative to individual and constituent characteristics? In answering these questions the chapter proceeds in three sections. The first section briefly motivates the study of Brazilian parties in light of both the historiography and the theory of policymaking in legisla-tures, with special emphasis on the economic significance of parti-san politics. The second section turns to empirical tests of party cohesion and partisan influence on voting outcomes in the Cham-ber of Deputies. The final section concludes.

Political Parties in Imperial Brazil: History and Theory

Historians of Brazilian political parties have generally assigned party a secondary role at best in legislative politics. Most correctly identify both the electoral connection and the influence of cabinets in shaping partisanship, but most also proclaim such partisanship to have been weak in the Parliament.[4] Curiously, none have actually

4. Graham, *Patronage and Politics*, pp. 149–60, passim; Emilia Viotti da Costa, *The Brazilian Empire* (Chicago: University of Chicago Press, 1985), pp. 69–72; Ro-derick J. Barman, *Citizen Emporer: Pedro Ii and the Making of Brazil, 1825–1891* (Stanford: Stanford University Press, 1999), pp. 172, 323. For a perspective that argues for the cohesion of parties but focuses on the socioeconomic origins of

attempted to measure the degree of party cohesion in legislative policymaking or searched systematically for other determinants of voting outcomes on the floor of the chamber. Political scientists have advanced a variety of explanations for the existence and strength of political parties in legislatures more generally, but none of these have been applied to nineteenth-century Brazil. These explanations range from teleological (parties may induce equilibrium policy outcomes) to purely rational and self-interested on the part of politicians (parties provide resources that legislative candidates value, ranging from funds for election campaigns to party labels that prove useful in providing electoral cues).[5] Whether parties are strong in a legislature, or not, is largely a function of the electoral mechanism. Low district magnitudes and winner-take-all elections, combined with disincentives to intraparty competition for votes, promote strong party organizations.[6] Add to those features a partly exogenous source of campaign resources, and one has the makings, in theory, of a very strong party.

Such features characterize the Brazilian polity in general, and the 1880s in particular quite well. Under Brazil's constitutional monarchy cabinets were hand selected by the emperor, not created by the parliamentary majority.[7] Since cabinets administered elections, they wielded enormous direct and indirect influence over electoral outcomes. Deputies of the majority party could ill afford to ignore the policy preferences of the cabinet, since the cabinet (usu-

---

partisans rather than parties per se, see José Murilo de Carvalho, *A Construção Da Ordem* and *Teatro De Sombras* (Rio de Janeiro: Editora UFRJ/Relume Dumará, 1996), p. 374.

5. John H. Aldrich, *Why Parties?* (Chicago: University of Chicago Press, 1995), pp. 40–71, provides a thorough survey on the theoretical origins and consequences of legislative parties.

6. Gary W. Cox and Matthew D. McCubbins, "Structure and Policy: The Institutional Determinants of Policy Outcomes," ms., 1996, pp. 34–35.

7. São Vicente, *Direito Publico Brazileiro*, pp. 227–56, discusses the constitutional powers granted cabinets in Brazil.

ally made up of prominent party leaders) commanded critical electoral resources. Moreover, the reform that preceded the elections of 1881 returned Brazil to an electoral division of a large number of single-member districts, as many as twenty in one province. This reduced tendencies toward intraparty competition for votes. Each party would typically field a single candidate in a district, who then faced no competition in the actual election from within his or her own party, and hence had little reason to set himself apart from her or his party. These two features together—party-based cabinets with influence over elections and many small, single-member districts—provide every reason to expect that Brazil had strong political parties in the 1880s, despite the claims to the contrary on the part of specialists on the era.

Although ascertaining the strength of Brazilian parties is a key concern of the rest of this chapter, the economic consequences of partisan politics are of special interest in the Brazilian setting and warrant some elaboration. Somewhat ironically, the starting point is with models that deduce away political parties in a distributive politics setting.[8] To garner some insights into the economic consequences of distributive politics, the policy outcomes of two different arrangements underpinning market interventions may be compared with the benchmark of economic efficiency. The efficient policy is that of standard benefit-cost analysis and yields a project scale (be it a vector of expenditures and tax rates or a level of regulation) that maximizes the social surplus given the economy's resources.

---

8. The discussion here draws heavily on Barry R. Weingast, Kenneth A. Shepsle, and Christopher Johnsen, "The Political Economy of Benefits and Costs: A Neoclassical Approach to Distributive Politics," *Journal of Political Economy* 89 (1981): 642–64. Ensuing articles, especially Kenneth A. Shepsle and Barry R. Weingast, "Political Preferences for the Pork Barrel: A Generalization," *American Journal of Political Science* 25 (1981): 96–111; and Kenneth A. Shepsle and Barry R. Weingast, "Political Solutions to Market Problems," *American Political Science Review* 78 (1984): 417–35, allowed to a greater degree for partisan influence in pork-barrel politics but still emphasized heavily consituent interests in policymaking.

The first political arrangement departs from the efficient social planner by partitioning and politicizing the benefits and costs of a market intervention. Expenditures that go to politically relevant constituents represent not only resource costs but also political benefits for the legislator that obtains them. This arrangement thus transforms economic benefits and costs into political benefits and costs (from the perspective of a unitary policymaker), reassigning one component of resource costs to the benefit side of the equation. The equilibrium policy intervention in this case exceeds the optimal level. The second arrangement simply extends this politicization of project benefits and costs by partitioning the unitary government into a set of electoral districts defined on an arbitrary administrative division, where each district has a legislator and where policy outcomes are determined by majority rule. Under these conditions, the policy outcome is on a scale of market intervention even greater than that of the first case, which was already beyond the efficient policy. Legislators maximizing their political support, rather than net economic benefits, fail to internalize the negative externalities arising from the policies induced by the interests of their constituents. The key comparative statistics result is that the degree of inefficiency of the legislators' preferences for intervention worsens with an increase in the number of legislative districts.[9]

Attenuating this distortionary and dissipative scenario is any feature that reduces the de facto (if not the de jure) number of districts. Political parties, in pursuing a goal favorable to party members, would internalize some of the negative externalities arising from unfettered political self-interest seeking on the part of individual legislators. For example, the majority party, by wielding electoral resources valued by legislators, could induce its members to take

9. Weingast et al., "The Political Economy of Benefits and Costs," appropriately label this corollary the "Law of $1/N$." As N, the number of districts, increases, the distance between the efficient policy and equilibrium policy grows.

into consideration the political benefits and costs of market interventions to other members of the party. Although this leaves the
number of legislative districts intact, it effectively reduces them insofar as they bear on the scale of the policy intervention. In the case
where politicians pursue policies in response not only to constituent
interests but also to partisan concerns, the policy outcome is somewhere between that of the unitary polity and that of the purely
distributive legislature. The policy consequence of going from a
nonpartisan legislature to one with strong parties is a movement of
the market intervention from the extreme case of pure pork in the
direction of economic efficiency. Strong legislative parties, when
they exist, limit the inefficiency of market interventions.

Party and Voting on the Floor of the
Chamber of Deputies

The evidence used to examine the role of political parties in
policy outcomes is the roll-call voting records of the eighteenth
legislature (1881–1884).[10] The published debates for these years
contain forty-one roll calls or divisions. Such a data set is extraordinarily small by the standards of the United States or the United
Kingdom. It nonetheless permits the identification of significant
patterns of voting, both by party and for individual legislators. The
roll calls range from disputes over the seating of individual deputies
for electoral reasons, to proposed taxes and subsidies, to several
confidence votes in various cabinets.[11] During the eighteenth legis-

10. These were extracted from Brazil (various years), and I believe represent this
population of roll calls for these years. The roll calls are only incompletely indexed
and thus required a page-by-page search in the Brazilian parliamentary debates to
find them all.
11. William R. Summerhill, "Party, Faction, and Policy in Imperial Brazil," ms.,
Stanford University, 2000, provides a detailed list and description of the roll-call
votes.

lature, the Liberals held 78 of the 122 seats and the Conservatives held the balance.[12] The sessions from 1881 through 1884 were marked by considerable conflict and instability, as several cabinets fell to nonconfidence votes, and the emancipation of slaves over sixty years of age became a major policy question in the chamber.[13]

Attempting to identify the influence of party in roll-call voting outcomes raises thorny interpretive issues. Although students of legislative politics frequently invoke the importance of party in empirical work, present theory and method do not permit a definitive test of party strength.[14] Indeed, since the tests for party strength turn out to be observationally equivalent with an absence of party discipline under some fairly weak assumptions, one cannot on the basis of roll-call voting patterns alone make an argument for the influence of party. Rather, party influence must be inferred, with less strength than might be hoped for, from both quantitative and qualitative evidence.

As a starting point it is important to establish whether party is a reasonable candidate for explaining roll-call voting outcomes in light of the evidence. Three different tests provide insights into the relationship between party affiliation and voting patterns on the floor of the Chamber of Deputies. The first of these measures is the

12. See Barão de Jorge João Dodsworth Javari, *Organizações E Programas Ministeriais*, 2d ed. (Rio de Janeiro: Ministerio da Justica e Negocios Interiors, 1962), p. 378, for the party totals and breakdown by province.

13. The politics of this period are detailed in Roger Frank Colson, "The Destruction of a Revolution Polity: Economy and Society in Brazil, 1750–1895" (Ph.D. diss., Princeton University, 1979), and, with special emphasis on the emancipation question, by Robert Edgar Conrad, *The Destruction of Brazilian Slavery, 1850–1888* (Berkeley: University of California Press, 1972).

14. This point is made convincingly by Keith Krehbiel, "Paradoxes of Parties in Congress," *Legislative Studies Quarterly* 24 (1999): 31–64; and Keith Krehbiel, "Party Discipline and Measures of Partisanship," *American Journal of Political Science* 44 (2000): 212–27.

index of likeness,[15] which gauges the extent to which the two parties took similar positions on each roll-call vote. Figure 4.1 presents the index on each of forty-one roll calls taken in the eighteenth legislature between 1881 and 1884.

The index of likeness, while displaying some variability, strongly suggests that there were fundamental differences between Liberals and Conservatives by the time a question was voted on the floor of the chamber. The vast majority of the divisions reveals low indices of likeness. In only one of the roll calls were the Liberals and Conservatives quite similar. But there the result is largely artifactual; a large number of Liberals boycotted the vote, in an apparent attempt to deny the chamber a quorum. Of those remaining, several sided with the Conservatives, giving rise to an unusually strong similarity between the parties.[16] Whether the typical difference between the Liberals and Conservatives was a result of the influence of their respective parties, or whether party affiliation itself was a result of their constituent interests of ideological positions, cannot be determined from the index.[17] Nonetheless, in their overall voting patterns, the parties were not indistinguishable, as some historians claim. On the contrary their differences were quite apparent.

A second test examines the degree of cohesiveness of each party. The measure employed is the index of cohesion, and its interpretation is straightforward.[18] The greater the proportion of legisla-

15. See Lee F. Anderson, Meredith W. Watts Jr., and Allen R. Wilcox, *Legislative Roll-Call Analysis* (Evanston, Ill.: Northwestern University Press, 1966), pp. 44–45.

16. A chi-square test for the strength of the association between party and a deputy's vote on each roll call proved to be significant for every roll call except this same one.

17. This because it suffers from precisely the problems identified by Krehbiel, "Party Discipline and Measures of Partisanship."

18. This is the Rice index; see Anderson et al., , *Legislative Roll-Call Analysis*, pp. 32–40. For a discussion of indices of cohesion in other historical settings, see Gary W. Cox, *The Efficient Secret: The Cabinet and the Development of Political Parties in*

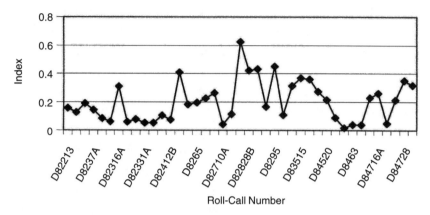

Figure 4.1   Index of Likeness for Liberals and Conservatives in Brazil's Chamber of Deputies, Eighteenth Legislature (1881–1884)

tors from a party who vote together, the higher the party's index. Figure 4.2 presents the index of cohesion for each of the parties across the 41 roll-call votes.

Although the Conservatives enjoyed greater cohesion than the majority party on average, cohesion for both parties was typically high. Liberals suffered greater defections but still exhibited an index of cohesion greater than 0.5 on more than 75 percent of the roll calls. Combined with the index of likeness, the index of cohesion supports the view that the parties were quite different from each other, while each was internally coherent.

A third test extends the first two by applying factor analysis to each roll call to first establish the major issues, or dimensions of conflict, and then to plot each deputy on those dimensions.[19] It then

Victorian England (Cambridge, England: Cambridge University Press, 1987), pp. 21–31.

19. A variety of techniques are available for such an estimate; see Anderson et al., *Legislative Roll-Call Analysis*, pp. 123–174; Keith T. Poole and Howard Rosenthal, "A Spatial Model for Legislative Roll-Call Analysis," *American Journal of Political Science* 29 (1985): 357–84; and James J. Heckman and James M. Snyder Jr., "Linear

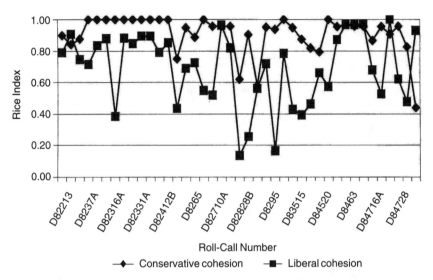

Figure 4.2   Rice Index of Party Cohesion for Liberals and Conservatives in Brazil's Chamber of Deputies, Eighteenth Legislature (1881–1884)

tests a variety of determinants of each deputy's position to include party, personal characteristics, and constituent characteristics. For the forty-one roll calls from the eighteenth legislature, one dimension of conflict accounts for the majority of the variance among the votes cast by deputies; a second dimension accounts for another 5 or so percent of the variance; and additional dimensions account for less still.[20] Figure 4.3 presents the unrotated factor loading plots for the roll calls, which by and large exhibits the desired pattern of roll calls lumping together on each end of the horizontal axis.

Figure 4.4 plots each deputy on the two most important factors, each of which represents an issue or dimension of conflict, much

Probability Models of the Demand for Attributes with an Empirical Application to Estimating the Preferences of Legislators," *RAND Journal of Economics* 28 (1997): S142–S189. Here I use the standard principal components version of factor analysis.

20.   Greater detail on the results of the factor analysis are in Summerhill, "Party, Faction, and Policy in Imperial Brazil."

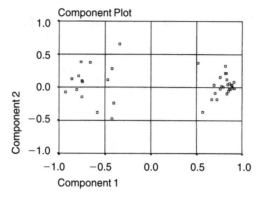

Figure 4.3   Factor Loading Plots for Forty-One Roll Call Votes in the Chamber of Deputies, 1881–1884

like a simple left-right political continuum. Visual inspection is sufficient to infer that party affiliation is closely related to each deputy's policy position on the first dimension since the Conservatives cluster to the left of the horizontal axis and Liberals cluster to the right, exhibiting virtually no overlap.

Whereas party affiliation is closely related to the first dimension, the second dimension holds no such simple interpretation since deputies from both parties are intermingled on the vertical axis. Regression analysis provides greater insight on the apparent strength of party on the first dimension and also allows an exploration of whether there are systematic determinants of the deputies' positions on the second dimension. Figure 4.5 presents the results of a regression where the dependent variable is a deputy's score on the first dimension and where the independent variables either capture or proxy party, occupational background, electoral strength, and constituent interest in the critical issue of the era, which was slavery.

The results are wholly consistent with the picture that emerges in Figure 4.4; party affiliation, far more than any other variable, accounts for each deputy's position on the first issue. Most occupa-

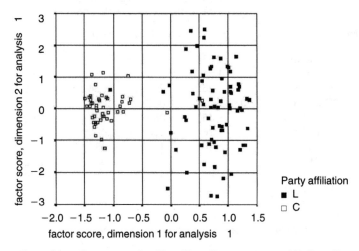

Figure 4.4   Legislator Scores on the First Two Dimensions of Policy Conflict in Brazil's Chamber of Deputies, 1881–1884

tional variables fail to take on any statistical significance at all. Judges, however, were systematically more "liberal" than can be explained by party affiliation alone. The significant result for military officers is idiosyncratic since only one deputy was classified as military. The defining feature of conflict on the first, and most important, dimension was partisan affiliation.

Figure 4.6 provides an identical analysis for the deputies on the second dimension of conflict but yields very different results.

Party affiliation plays no role whatsoever in the deputies' respective positions on the second dimension; nor do any of the occupational variables. The only two variables that take on statistical significance are a provincewide measure of constituent interest in slavery (the number of slaves per elector in the province) and the margin by which the deputy won the last election.[21] Although the

21. Data derived from Barão de Jorge João Dodsworth Javari, *Organizações E Programas Ministeriais*, 2d ed. (Rio de Janeiro, Ministerio da Justica e Negocios Interiors, 1962), pp. 373–378. The number of slaves refers to figures from 1872; see

Coefficients [a]

Model	Unstandardized Coefficients		Standardized Coefficients	t	Sig.
	B	Std. Error	Beta		
1 (Constant)	−1.056	.088		−12.068	.000
PARTY	1.897	.068	.931	27.911	.000
BIZNESS	.265	.252	.034	1.054	.294
DOCTOR	9.660E-02	.087	.037	1.114	.268
ENGINEER	−.355	.353	−.032	−1.005	.317
FARMER	.267	.253	.034	1.055	.294
JUDGE	.400	.164	.080	2.437	.016
MATH	.204	.182	.037	1.122	.265
MILITARY	−1.862	.352	−.170	−5.291	.000
SLAVELEC	−1.03E-02	.007	−.049	−1.460	.147
MARGIN2	−5.39E-03	.005	−.036	−1.068	.288

[a] Dependent Variable: factor score, dimension 1 for analysis 1

Model Summary

Model	R	R Square	Adjusted R Square	Std. Error of the Estimate
1	.944 [a]	.891	.881	.3461554

[a] Predictors: (Constant), MARGIN2, MATH, ENGINEER, BIZNESS, MILITARY, FARMER, JUDGE, DOCTOR, PARTY, SLAVELEC

Figure 4.5   Determinants of Deputies' Scores on the First Dimension of Conflict.   *Note:* The dependent variable is the deputy's factor score on the first dimension. Party is a dummy variable equal to 1 when the deputy was a Liberal and zero otherwise. All the remaining independent variables except the last two are dummy variables for the deputy's occupation. BIZNESS indicates a merchant, and MATH a mathematics professor. DOCTOR, ENGINEER, FARMER, JUDGE, and MILITARY are literal labels. The default occupation is an attorney. SLAVELEC is the number of slaves per elector in the deputy's province (not his district). MARGIN2 is the percentage margin of victory the deputy enjoyed in the previous election. For a more detailed explanation of this analysis see William R. Summerhill, "Party, Faction, and Policy in Imperial Brazil" (ms., Stanford University, 2000).   *Sources:* Factor scores are derived from the procedure discussed in the text. Party affiliation, occupational variables, number of electors, and the electoral margin are derived from Barão de Jorge João Dodsworth Javari, *Organizações E Programas Ministeriais,* 2d ed. (Rio de Janeiro: Ministerio da Justica e Negocios Interiors, 1962), pp. 373–78. The number of slaves refers to figures from 1872; see Robert Edgar Conrad, *The Destruction of Brazilian Slavery, 1850–1888* (Berkeley: University of California Press, 1972), p. 300.

Coefficients [a]

Model	Unstandardized Coefficients		Standardized Coefficients		
	B	Std. Error	Beta	t	Sig.
1 (Constant)	.744	.244		3.054	.003
PARTY	2.639E-03	.189	.001	.014	.989
BIZNESS	.117	.702	.015	.167	.868
DOCTOR	−5.53E-02	.242	−.021	−.229	.819
ENGINEER	−.367	.983	−.033	−.374	.709
FARMER	3.674E-02	.704	.005	.052	.958
JUDGE	−.214	.457	−.043	−.467	.641
MATH	−.420	.507	−.075	−.829	.409
MILITARY	5.610E-02	.980	.005	.057	.954
SLAVELEC	−5.85E-02	.020	−.276	−2.974	.004
MARGIN2	−3.89E-02	.014	−.260	−2.769	.007

[a] Dependent Variable: factor score, dimension 1 for analysis 1

Model Summary

Model	R	R Square	Adjusted R Square	Std. Error of the Estimate
1	.394 [a]	.155	.078	.9643864

[a] Predictors: (Constant), MARGIN2, MATH, ENGINEER, BIZNESS, MILITARY, FARMER, JUDGE, DOCTOR, PARTY, SLAVELEC

Figure 4.6   Determinants of Deputies' Scores on the Second Dimension of Conflict.   *Note:* The dependent variable is the deputy's factor score on the second dimension. Party is a dummy variable equal to 1 when the deputy was a Liberal and zero otherwise. All the remaining independent variables except the last two are dummy variables for the deputy's occupation. BIZNESS indicates a merchant, and MATH a mathematics professor. DOCTOR, ENGINEER, FARMER, JUDGE, and MILITARY are literal labels. The default occupation is an attorney. SLAVELEC is the number of slaves per elector in the deputy's province (not his district). MARGIN2 is the percentage margin of victory the deputy enjoyed in the previous election. For a more detailed explanation of this analysis see William R. Summerhill, "Party, Faction, and Policy in Imperial Brazil" (ms., Stanford University, 2000).   *Sources:* Factor scores are derived from the procedure discussed in the text. Party affiliation, occupational variables, number of electors, and the electoral margin are derived from Barão de Jorge João Dodsworth Javari, *Organizações E Programas Ministeriais,* 2d ed. (Rio de Janeiro: Ministerio da Justica e Negocios Interiors, 1962), pp. 373–78. The number of slaves refers to figures from 1872; see Robert Edgar Conrad, *The Destruction of Brazilian Slavery, 1850–1888* (Berkeley: University of California Press, 1972), p. 300.

magnitude of the effect is small, the results indicate that the second dimension was some combination of direct constituent interest in the slavery question and the electoral "slack" enjoyed by the deputy.

The three tests here are suggestive: voting on the floor was quite consistent with the deputies' party affiliation. As already stated, such tests are not definitive because party affiliation can have two distinct components: party discipline imposed by party organization and leaders and the selection effect, whereby deputies that are already partisan in response to their constituents' interests, or ideology, sort themselves into two parties. None of the tests here can distinguish between these two possibilities. Although there is ample reason to believe that both components were at work in explaining the partisan pattern of voting, the party discipline model quite likely proved dominant in Brazil by 1881. Conservatives and Liberals indeed differed greatly in their underpinning viewpoints about the appropriate role of government, the division of authority between central and provincial governments, and the future course of policy, as exhibited in the party platforms and statements of principles.[22] As such, party affiliation depended on a form of ideological sorting on the part of individual deputies. Yet party organizations, thanks to the party identity of the cabinet, also wielded tremendous electoral influence. This influence was of much more proximate concern for the typical deputy than a statement of principles adopted, in the case of the Conservative party, decades earlier. Thus, by 1881 the factors discussed above that lead to strong parties were all in place in Brazil. Relatively small, single-member electoral districts, the cohesive nature of intraparty voting, the influence of partisan cabinets,

Robert Edgar Conrad, *The Destruction of Brazilian Slavery, 1850–1888* (Berkeley: University of California Press, 1972), p. 300.

22. Americo Brasiliense de Almeida e Melo, *Os Programas Dos Partidos E O Segundo Imperio* (Brasilia: Senado Federal, 1979).

and the observed differences between members of the two parties on roll-call votes, lead almost inexorably to the conclusion that Brazil enjoyed strong parties while still allowing for factional departures from a pure party model. Importantly, in a highly centralized polity, the economic impact of policymaking under strong parties created fewer distortions than if the chamber had operated in a nonpartisan manner.

Conclusion

In light of the abbreviated results reported here, it is no longer possible to dismiss the policy influence of the political parties of imperial Brazil. In contrast to the claims of historians, there is ample evidence that the Liberal and Conservative parties both differed from each other in their voting behavior and also exhibited a high degree of intraparty coherence. Rejecting the received wisdom does not mean that its polar opposite was true by default because party strength is not a dichotomous variable but rather a continuous one, which no doubt varied in its importance, both within specific legislatures and across sessions.[23] By avoiding inquiry informed by positive political theory, and systematic empirical work, historians of Brazilian politics failed to identify the salient dimensions of policy conflict in the chamber, the relative importance of those dimensions at different points in time, and the underpinning pattern of party voting. Brazilian parties cohered, albeit imperfectly, and differed on the most fundamental dimension of policymaking. Cronyism, or the politics of patronage, and its economic consequences in imperial Brazil can no longer be understood without reference to the politics of parties.

---

23. A conjecture that remains to be investigated, but that is consistent with features of the Brazilian case, is that earlier episodes of multimember electoral districts weakened party discipline in the chamber.

Economic Crises and
Reform in Mexico

In 1979, one of the oil boom years, President Lopez Portillo announced Mexico's intention to adhere to the General Agreement on Tariffs and Trade (GATT). He then reversed this decision in 1980, having engaged in consultations with major interest groups. Under President de la Madrid (1982–88), Mexico experienced several negative shocks, namely, the collapse of the price of oil and the interruption of foreign credit influx at a time when around 5 percent of the GDP was being used to service foreign debt. To make matters worse, the country suffered one of the most severe earthquakes of the century. Even in the midst of these crises, in 1985 Mexico acceded to GATT. By 1987, it had transformed itself from an extremely closed economy into one of the most open in the world. In 1993, it signed the North American Free Trade Agreement (NAFTA) with Canada and the United States. This transformation occurred notwithstanding the fact that trade liberalization implied significant adjustment costs for the private, import-competing sector and that the state-owned sector had seen its subsidies vanish as a result. Nonetheless, the import-competing sector, which had opposed trade liberalization in 1979, did not oppose it in 1985. It is curious that it should have been President de la Madrid, typically portrayed as weak and indecisive, to initiate the change, rather than President Lopez Portillo, who was seen as a strong leader.

Following the liberalization of trade, the government implemented a far-reaching fiscal reform. The majority of state-owned companies were privatized, bringing their number down from 1,155 in 1982 to fewer than 220 in 1993; the income tax rate was reduced from 42 percent to 34 percent, and tax compliance was enforced, resulting in increased tax collection; and government subsidies were significantly reduced. These reforms changed the sign of the primary fiscal balance from negative during the period 1970–82 to positive for each year of the period 1983–93. It is worth noting that the reform took place in a context of deteriorating terms of trade. The index of the terms of trade fell around 50 percent between 1981 and 1986.

The Mexican reforms and other reforms that occur in the context described above raise the following questions: Why is it that power holders do not block such reforms, even though all or most of them result in conditions worse than the status quo? Why do such reforms happen in the aftermath of a crisis and not during good times, when the country might be able to afford the short-term costs more easily? Finally, why do power holders allow the economy to reach a state of crisis?

The objective of this chapter is to address these questions for the case of Mexico.

To facilitate this discussion, it is useful to think of the economy as being composed of two sectors: the organized elite and the rest of the population. In the unreformed status quo, organized groups extract rents from the rest of the economy. Economic reform is a set of structural changes that eliminates the power of some or all of these groups. These changes need not enhance efficiency for the economy as a whole (as would be the case with privatization or trade liberalization) but may simply consist of expropriations or a move toward protectionism.

I classify the explanations for why reform occurs into two frameworks. In one scenario, called *barbarians at the gate*, reform is imposed by forces external to the organized elite. In the second framework, termed *reform from within*, privileged groups themselves induce the reforms. A common barbarians-at-the-gate explanation is that a severe crisis leads voters to replace the current government and vote for reform. Another explanation is that during a crisis governments are forced to ask for assistance from multilateral institutions and that help comes under the condition that a reform is implemented. Although external factors are important, an explanation of reform based solely on them does not seem appropriate for cases such as the radical trade liberalizations that took place in Chile (1975) and Mexico (1985). Neither President de la Madrid nor General Augusto Pinochet faced pressure from voters or exporters to open up the economy and destroy a big part of the inefficient manufacturing sector. In these cases, reform was induced by the powerful elites.

Next, I consider the reform-from-within framework. One commonly used argument is that, during a crisis, powerful groups decide to abandon the status quo because the situation is so bad that a majority of powerful groups expect to benefit from reform. This argument, however, does little to illuminate the reforms we are trying to rationalize. These reforms do not take place in a smooth environment but rather in the midst of political turmoil, in which some or all powerful groups are displaced from power and suffer substantial economic losses.

A Reform-from-within Explanation

I present an argument in which reform serves as a tool to limit the power of political opponents. In the next section I apply the argument to Mexico. I consider an economy in which powerful groups with common access to the economy's resources find it individually rational to overappropriate resources. As a result, there is a deterioration of the economy. When the economy reaches a crisis, a conflict among powerful groups erupts, the result of which is a reform that can leave all groups worse off than before.

In my model, reform occurs if one or more groups unilaterally relinquishes its privileges. Any group that undertakes this action must reallocate its fixed assets, which entails costs for the group in question because it has to divert part of its assets to nonproductive activities during the transition. The long-term benefit is that the postreform regime will be more favorable toward this group than it would otherwise be. In equilibrium, the group (call it i) that introduces the change ends up worse off than in the status quo. Why, then, would i induce reform? It does so either to prevent other groups from introducing changes that would harm i even more or to neutralize the harmful effects of changes already introduced by other groups.

To illustrate this point, consider a group of protected producers who receive production subsidies and have the power to block or introduce trade liberalization. In the short run, trade liberalization is costly for these producers because their fixed assets must be reallocated. However, the institutions, such as trade agreements, that develop over the long run will weaken unions and statist groups. As a result, exporters will have the upper hand. As I discuss in the section on Chile, the protected producers in Chile and Mexico supported trade liberalization to stop expropriations by labor and statist groups, respectively. It should be clear that protected producers would have preferred the status quo. However, the alternative to trade liberalization was not the status quo but expropriation by rival groups.

When the economy is doing well, every group finds that the short-run diversion of resources to nonproductive activities is more costly than the future benefits it might gain. Therefore, every group would be better off by not introducing a change to neutralize the changes introduced by others (i.e., becoming the follower), than by introducing a change unilaterally (i.e., becoming the leader). In these circumstances any reform is unanimously blocked by all groups, and rent seeking flourishes. As the economy deteriorates, however, there is a fall in the opportunity cost of diverting productive factors to destroy the power of the rival groups. Thus, there is a point in time after which each group prefers to be the leader instead of the follower. Although every group would prefer to have a reform far in the future, a preemptive reform inevitably takes place much earlier, given each group's perspective that the other groups would stay put forever. This is when leading becomes preferred to following. That is, group i will introduce a reform to prevent other groups from introducing changes that will harm group i. The ultimate result is that all groups end up worse off than before.

Modeling this interdependence is, in principle, complicated. On the one hand, the timing of reform depends on the state of the economy. On the other hand, the state of the economy is a function of the powerful groups' past appropriative behavior, which in turn is a function of the expected reform date. In equilibrium, the appropriation policies and the reform date must be mutually consistent. A contribution of this chapter is to present a dynamic game in which this interdependence is explicitly taken into account.

We should recognize that the correct explanation for reform is a combination of the reform-from-within and barbarians-at-the-gate views. Nonetheless, the model presented in this chapter is useful because it introduces factors previously neglected in the study of reform, namely, the role of crises, the intraelite conflict, and the use of reform as a tool to limit the power of political opponents.[1]

---

1. A popular explanation for the Mexican reform is that it took place in the aftermath of the debt crisis because the IMF forced Mexico to open as a precondition for lending it more money. Note, however, that the same pressure was faced by Brazil and Peru, yet neither liberalized in the 1980s. Like Brazil and Peru, Mexico could have declared a moratorium and followed with inward-looking policies. Mexico chose not to pursue this path. Although there is no question that the IMF and the World Bank have played important roles, "it would be a mistake to picture the

The Mexican Experience

I address the following questions about the Mexican reforms: First, why did trade liberalization take place in the economically and politically strained environment of the 1980s instead of during the oil boom years, when Mexico could more easily have afforded such a reform? Second, why did the Salinas government pursue NAFTA so feverishly? What were the expected gains from accession, given that Mexico had already liberalized trade in manufacturing, that U.S. tariff levels were quite low, and that NAFTA entailed significant costs? Third, why didn't the government completely open trade in agriculture and services early on, given that this measure would have reduced input prices and made manufactures more competitive? More generally, hoping to derive broad lessons from the Mexican reform process, in particular, I address the questions of when trade liberalization is most likely to take place, under which conditions it is most likely to be sustainable, and what the role of a formal agreement like NAFTA is in sustaining a reform process.

I first present a brief historical overview to put the Mexican reform process in perspective. The Mexican political system centers on a president who has many formal powers but cannot be reelected and on an official party (first called PNR, then PMR, and now PRI) that, until the elections of 2000, had won every presidential election for the last sixty years. The Mexican president, however, is by no means an all-powerful autocrat. Nor is the PRI a monolithic party in which every member follows the president's instructions. The roots of this political structure can be found in the process of

---

process of policy reform as one where orthodox economic policies were externally imposed on unwilling policymakers." In fact, "more often than not, reform has had a significant home-grown component exceeding World Bank expectations and stipulations" (Dany Rodrick, "Understanding Economic Policy Reform," *Journal of Economic Literature* 34 [1996]: 9–44).

Mexico's state formation. During the 1920s, Mexico was basically in a state of anarchy: several powerful local elites and armies held the control over each region. After President-elect Alvaro Obregón was assassinated in 1929, then President Calles formed the PNR as an emergency agreement with powerful groups and local bosses across the country to comply with the formalities of presidential elections.[2] In several states the existing bosses (*caciques*) and parties agreed to franchise the PNR name but did not yield any effective power to the central government. The state of Chiapas is a clear example.

The process of state formation, which paralleled the formation of the official party, consisted of transforming the independent local armies and power groups of each region into members of a national corporation. To induce them to accept this corporation, the government conferred on these groups monopoly rights over certain industries and/or geographic areas in exchange for loyalty. This consolidation process was enforced by an aggressive industrialization policy centered on import substitution and the undertaking of large infrastructure projects that generated significant rents for these groups. In addition the government granted generous tax exemptions and implemented favorable wage policies.

President Cárdenas (who served from 1934 to 1940) took this corporation process one step farther. First, he implemented an ambitious land reform through the Ejido program. This program gave the right to use land (but not ownership) to a vast number of peasants and absorbed the defeated peasant movements (Zapatistas) into the political corporation, minimizing the risk of future rebellions.[3] Second, the government gained control of the labor move-

2. See L. Meyer, "Los Inicios de la Institucionalizacion: La Politica del Maximato," in *Historia de la Revolution Mexicana*, vol. 12 (Mexico City: El Colegio de Mexico, 1978).

3. The *ejido* is a communal tenure system that prohibits the selling of land. This program limits peasants' access to credit and improvements in production and, in the long run, undermines agricultural productivity. Ultimately, the rural sector was

ment through the Confederacion de Trabajadores Mexicanos (CTM), which is still a pillar of the PRI. Lastly, the military was incorporated into the party.[4]

These policies generated social peace and high growth from the 1940s through the 1960s. A by-product was the entrenchment of powerful rent-seeking groups. By the late sixties one could distinguish two elites in the manufacturing sector: the private import-competing elite and the statist elite. In addition, the regional bosses who controlled the PRI voting machine and distributed government subsidies to the production of agricultural products comprised a rural elite. The statist elite was made up of networks associated with state-owned enterprises, such as managers, union leaders, and suppliers.

By powerful group or elite I refer to a group of people who control some fixed factors. Throughout the chapter I identify a group by the type of fixed factors it controls, not by the names of the people who comprise it. Thus, even if a group is destroyed, its members may remain powerful as part of a new group.

I turn now to the puzzle of why trade was not liberalized during the seventies, when it was considered necessary and when economic conditions could have supported it, but was instead enacted in the midst of the economic crisis of the mideighties. As discussed above, the political system in Mexico is such that no president had the autonomy to liberalize trade by decree since such liberalization implied the dismantling of a major part of the apparatus that generated rents for the strong elites. Therefore, in rationalizing trade liberalization events, we must bear in mind

---

polarized into two sectors, a modern and highly productive agricultural sector, with large-scale operation and access to export markets, and a backward sector formed mainly by ejido lands that remained isolated and scarcely linked to the market economy.

4. See A. Hernandez-Chavez, *La Mecanica Cárdenista. Historia de la Revoltion Mexicana*, vol. 16 (Mexico: El Colegio de Mexico, 1979).

that government actions do not reflect only the will of an all-powerful autocrat, nor are they solely determined by the will of a majority of atomistic voters. In addition to those of the president and the people, the interests of powerful elites exert a major influence over government actions. In all likelihood, all three interests influence most political events. In this chapter, however, I will emphasize the role of powerful elites. That is, I will explain the events in Mexico solely as the outcome of a game among powerful elites. I will assume that the president can take action and implement reform only if it is not blocked by powerful local elites.

As mentioned above, in the 1960s, 1970s, and 1980s, there were two strong groups within the Mexican manufacturing sector: the private import-competing elite and the statist elite. The political process guaranteed both elites almost unlimited access to fiscal revenue. They enjoyed subsidized inputs and profited from convoluted regulations and strict trade barriers, which increased the profitability of the fixed factors they owned. So why didn't these manufacturing sector elites unanimously block trade liberalization in the economically strained eighties as they had done during the seventies boom? The argument by Tornell[5] addresses this issue—the following is a summary of that argument.

To understand the process that led to trade liberalization, think of both the private import-competing elite and the statist elite as interacting in a preemption game. At every instant, each group has the opportunity to eliminate the other group's power by incurring a once-and-for-all cost. The group that incurs this cost becomes the leader and attains the power to monopolize fiscal transfers in the future. The other group becomes the follower and loses all claim to

5. Aaron Tornell, "Are Economic Crises Necessary for Trade Liberalization and Fiscal Reform? The Mexican Experience," in R. Dornbusch and S. Edwards, eds., *Reform, Recovery, and Growth* (Chicago: University of Chicago Press, 1995).

future fiscal transfers. If both groups incur the cost simultaneously (i.e., if they match), both see their power to extract fiscal revenue diminished, but neither loses relative to the other. The cohabitation equilibrium that sustains the status quo breaks down when the payoff of becoming the leader exceeds the payoff of maintaining the status quo. Moreover, if the payoff of matching is greater than the payoff of following, then each group weakens the other. In this case the government becomes relatively autonomous and is no longer beholden to elites. Therefore, it becomes free to implement a reform.

But when does the payoff of becoming the leader exceed the payoff of remaining in the status quo? To address this issue I note that all payoffs are functions of the fiscal revenue available for redistribution. As fiscal revenue declines, the marginal utility of gaining a greater share of it increases. Thus the payoff of leading increases relative to the payoff of remaining in the status quo, and the payoff of matching increases relative to following. For a sufficiently large decline in fiscal revenue, the payoff of leading becomes greater than the payoff of the status quo, and the payoff of matching becomes greater than the payoff of following. As a result each group tries to displace the other in order to get a greater share of the lower fiscal revenue. Hence, when fiscal revenue is low, the status quo collapses and the potential for reform exists.

Now let us apply this argument to the Mexican experience of the 1970s and 1980s. After the students' riot of 1968, the government of President Echeverria (president from 1970 to 1976) tried to reestablish legitimacy and assuage demands for a reduction in poverty and income inequality by expanding public investment. This expansion significantly strengthened the statist elite. Although Echeverria had a strong antibusiness rhetoric, he did not take any measure to reduce the rents received by the private import-substituting elite. For instance, in 1971 he tried to implement a tax reform to increase tax revenues, which made up 8 percent of GDP. However, he soon abandoned that move. Also, in 1973 Echeverria enacted a law that limited foreign investment, benefiting the private elite.

Echeverria's antibusiness rhetoric created a strain between the government and the private sector. President Lopez Portillo, elected in 1976, set out to relieve this strain. After the 1977 discovery of significant oil reserves, and after the price of oil had increased, the government enacted a free-for-all fiscal policy that benefited both elites. The increase in fiscal transfers showed up in the form of an increase in government expenditures from 10 percent of GDP in 1970 to 22 percent in 1982. An example of increased transfers to the private sector was the 1981 half-billion-dollar bailout of Grupo Alfa, the biggest private company in Mexico at the time. Other specific actions funded by the expansion included the acceleration of the investment program in government-owned enterprises, the subsidization of oil, gas, and electricity prices, and the establishment of an ambitious antipoverty program, the Mexican Alimentary System (SAM). SAM, which supported grain production and was intended to benefit the poorest citizens of Mexico, provided subsidies that were mostly captured by the rural elite.[6] Lopez Portillo's expansionary policies caused the fiscal deficit to jump from 10 percent of GDP in 1977 to 17 percent in 1982.

During the 1970s, fiscal revenue remained high enough to finance all this additional government spending. Government subsidies increased the probability of fixed factors owned by the statist elite and the private import-substituting elite. The elites were satisfied with the transfers they were receiving, so no powerful group had incentive to push for the structural reforms that were needed. During the boom years of the 1970s no group found that the benefit

---

6. J. Fox, "Political Change in Mexico's New Peasant Economy," in Cook et al., eds., *The Politics of Economic Restructuring* (San Diego: University of California Press, 1994).

of ensuring itself a large share of future fiscal revenue outweighed the short-run costs of weakening the other groups. Therefore, all powerful elites unanimously blocked reform during those years.

During the eighties, falling oil prices and an interruption in foreign lending forced cutbacks in Mexico's generous government transfer programs—fiscal revenue could no longer cover the demands of all interest groups. This reduction in the size of the pie increased the marginal utility of gaining a greater share of it, and increased the payoff of becoming the leader (recall the preemption game discussed above).

The statist elite made the first move, inducing the government to expropriate all Mexican private banks. The banks channeled much fiscal revenue to the private sector (through subsidized credit and implicit guarantees of their borrowing from foreign banks), and their owners comprised one of the strongest groups in the private elite. Lopez Portillo announced the banks' expropriation in September 1982, three months before he left office, in a dramatic address to Congress during which he cried over his failure to help the poor.[7] Alongside the expropriation of the banks, capital controls were imposed and Miguel Mancera, orthodox governor of Mexico's Central Bank, resigned. The private sector responded to these blows by announcing that a national strike would take place on September 8, but representatives canceled the strike a few days later.

The private import-competing elite matched the statist elite's first move. Aware that trade liberalization would be a mechanism by which it could destroy the power of the statist elite, the private elite did not oppose the liberalization in the 1980s as it had in the 1970s. This time, the private elite's choice was not between trade

7. It has been argued that the banks' expropriation was really a bailout. Indeed, the banking system was insolvent and the government took over all its liabilities. However, the point I want to stress in this chapter is that the bankers lost the right to operate banks and thus lost access to future bailouts, as well as the right to obtain other types of fiscal transfers.

liberalization and the protectionist status quo, but between trade liberalization and becoming the follower, which would mean being further expropriated by the statist elite. When President de la Madrid took office in December 1982, members of the private elite feared that under his tenure expropriations would continue and statism would increase. After all, he had been minister of budget and planning under Lopez Portillo and had budgeted the massive increase in investment in state-owned enterprises. Moreover, de la Madrid assumed the presidency before the Thatcher and Reagan revolutions repopularized free-market policies.

Trade liberalization has been painful for the private sector in that it has forced many firms into bankruptcy and has forced fixed factors to be reallocated, both of which have generated short-run adjustment costs. In addition, the private elite has lost the rents from protection it received before liberalization. Because of reallocation, it has also suffered from the loss of political power associated with the ownership of fixed factors in well-established industries. The extent of these reallocation costs was illustrated in the previous section.

Despite these drawbacks for the private elite, trade liberalization could drastically reduce the power of the statist elite to further expropriate the private elite and extract fiscal subsidies. This would occur through three channels. First, free trade would create new powerful groups of exporters and foreign investors with incentives to defend the new status quo. Thus, an expropriation would not only draw opposition from these new export groups but also from foreigners. Since the potential cost of confronting powerful foreign firms would be high, it is unlikely that the government would engage in further expropriation. Second, free trade abolished the complex system of import licensing and multiple tariffs, replacing it with one or two rates that apply across the board. This more transparent system quickly highlights rent-seeking behavior, allowing other groups to block such behavior right away. Third, agreements signed by a country as part of trade liberalization (such as GATT and NAFTA) impose limits on the extent of subsidization to specific industries and rent-generating regulations that a government can impose.

Ultimately, both elites became weaker and worse off after the expropriation of the banks and trade liberalization. It is important to note that there was no uncertainty beforehand that this would happen. Both groups induced this outcome because, as a result of decreased government revenue in the early 1980s, the payoff of unilaterally deviating from the status quo at that time by trying to become the leader exceeded the payoff of maintaining the status quo. (Note that the Coase Theorem does not apply in this case because there is no third party with the power to enforce an agreement between two elites.)

Once each group in the manufacturing sector had weakened the other, the de la Madrid and Salinas governments attained relative autonomy. They used this autonomy to implement a tax reform, a radical privatization program, and a deregulation program that eliminated many privileges and monopolies conferred during the consolidating years of the PRI.

The puzzling point I wish to highlight and the one I will try to rationalize is that these governments did not fully liberalize agriculture and services. From an economic standpoint, this is an incongruity. If a government's objective is to promote manufactured exports, the proper policy is to liberalize agriculture and services. Liberalizing agriculture would free unskilled labor and reduce unskilled wages. Liberalizing services would reduce interest rates, transport costs, and communication costs. Since unskilled labor and services are inputs in the manufacture of exports, the government would certainly promote exports by liberalizing agriculture and services, thereby driving down the costs of these inputs.

Why did the two governments choose not to follow such obviously advantageous policies? My next point is that the decision not to open trade in agriculture and services fully was entirely necessary to ensure that the reform process would not be derailed. Reformers needed two things to continue pursuing reform. First, they had to be reelected, which could be difficult given that initially the reform did not have much support in the population. Second, they had to avoid alienating all powerful groups simultaneously. With respect to the first requirement, reelection, the reformers depended heavily on the rural vote in the 1988 and 1994 presidential elections because reforms in the manufacturing sector had damaged the urban electoral machine and elections in urban areas had become more contested. With respect to the second requirement, delaying liberalization of agriculture and services allowed the government to avoid alienating all powerful elites simultaneously, while building new elites to support the new strategy of export promotion and private property.

Let us elaborate on the first requirement, the issue of reelection. A few months before the presidential elections of 1988, some members of the statist elite who had spun off from the PRI combined with leftist parties to form the Partido de la Revolution Democratica (PRD) and captured a third of the vote. Also, the private elite increased its involvement in politics following the 1982 expropriation of the banks. This involvement broke the private elite's implicit agreement with the government by which the private elite stayed out of politics and the government in turn ensured a profitable investment climate.[8] As a result, elections in urban areas became more contested. Therefore, the PRI has had to rely more on the rural electoral machine to win presidential elections. For instance, Salinas, who received 50.5 percent of the total vote, won only 34.0 percent of the vote in "very urban" areas, while he received 77.0

8. S. Maxfield and R. Anzaldua, eds., *Government and Private Sector in Contemporary Mexico* (San Diego: University of California Press, 1987).

percent in "very rural" areas.[9] The rural electoral machine is closely linked to the network that administers protection to the agricultural sector. Opening trade in agriculture and thus dismantling this protectionist network might have destroyed the rural machine and, with it, the presidential hopes of reformers like Salinas and Zedillo.

To expand on the second requirement above, one can view the second part of the de la Madrid administration and the Salinas administration as having been devoted to creating new elites that would support the export promotion and private property strategy. Two new elites were formed under these administrations: the private export elite and the foreign investors elite. Deregulation, privatization, and new rules for foreign direct investment (FDI) were used as instruments in promoting these elites. Deregulation eliminated the convoluted rules that allowed some groups to enjoy monopoly rents.[10] Through privatization, the government transferred to the new private elite virtually all the firms in the manufacturing sector, with the exception of the energy sector. Through less discretionary rules the government attracted a significantly greater amount of FDI than it had historically. These actions further weakened both the statist elite and the old private import-competing elite.

Several investors who had not been in the big leagues during the 1970s and 1980s were able to acquire government assets which transformed them into what one might call "new strong groups." The steel industry illustrates this point. Before privatization there was only one private integrated steel producer in Mexico—Hylsa (a subsidiary of Alfa, beneficiary of the 1981 bailout discussed above). After the privatization of the steel sector, the relative power of Alfa

9. See J. Fox, footnote 6.
10. A. Fernandez, "Deregulation as a Source of Growth in Mexico," in R. Dornbusch and S. Edwards, eds., *Reform, Recovery, and Growth* (Chicago: University of Chicago Press, 1995).

diminished drastically—now it is only one among five major steel producers. The others are GAN, a consortium of a former pharmaceutical group, a small mining group, and a Dutch steel producer; IMSA, a group of former medium-sized steel producers; ISPAT, a group from India; and Villaccro, a group of former medium-sized steel traders. It is interesting to note that as a response to the increased competition induced by privatization, Alfa recently opened a new steel plant that is internationally competitive. Before privatization, it is likely that Alfa would simply have sought more protection and received it, threatening to close down if it did not.

Today, shutdown threats from a single steel producer could not effectively induce protection because other domestic producers are available to fill the employment and production gap a shutdown would create. An example of this new regime is the recent bankruptcy of AHMSA, the largest steel producer in Mexico. In early 1999 the government refused to bail out the company when it declared that it could not meet its debt service on nearly two billion dollars.

Another indicator of the dilution of power within the private elite that Salinas's reforms have brought about is the increased number of Mexican billionaires. According to *Forbes* magazine, there was only one billionaire family in Mexico in the late 1980s—the Garza Sada family, Alfa's major shareholder. In 1994, there were twenty-four Mexican billionaires, according to *Forbes*. Outstanding examples are Roberto Gonzalez, Carlos Slim, and Salinas Pliego. Gonzalez developed the market for tortilla flour and is the biggest producer of tortillas in the United States. In the recent privatization of the banks he acquired Banorte. Slim controls Telefonos de Mexico, the telephone monopoly, in association with Southwestern Bell and France Telecom. Salinas Pliego is the top Mexican retailer of household appliances. He recently bought from the government Television Azteca, which has a joint venture with NBC, making him the only private competitor of Televisa, Mexico's other television network. It is worth noting that ten years ago none of these families were billionaires — they did not even rank among the country's richest.

I should clarify that the new elite was not totally formed by newcomers; in fact, many of its members had familial or historical links to the old elite. The important point is that the new group is defined not by the historical background of its members but by their interest in defending the new set of property rights. This common interest is in turn determined by the fact that they own and control fixed factors whose profitability depends on exports.

Summing up, the policies followed by the government during the period 1985–1994 (trade liberalization, deregulation, opening to foreign direct investment, and privatization) had the effect of weakening the statist elite and the private import-competing elite and inducing the formation of two new powerful groups: the export elite and foreign investors. Since these new elites will benefit from the new set of property rights that have been imposed, once their power is consolidated, in the near future they are likely to expend resources to ensure that these property rights are maintained.

We should emphasize that the executive has played a critical role in this process as a coalition builder, not as an authoritarian central planner. This does not mean that the administrations of de la Madrid and Salinas did not push hard for unpopular policies designed to establish the new property rights regime that would support an efficient export economy. Important examples of their efforts in this direction are the tax reform, the privatization program, and the deregulation program.

Next, I try to rationalize President Salinas's willingness to incur such high political costs in order to ensure NAFTA's approval by the U.S. Congress. Under NAFTA, trade liberalization in services and agriculture was not going to be immediate but would happen gradually over the following ten to fifteen years. This gradual liberalization would be a blow to the elite associated with traditional agriculture, who derive their power from the distribution of subsidies to inefficient producers. This is a serious concern because the PRI vote comes largely from rural voters, and to a great extent the agricultural elite controls the machine that produces this vote. Thus, trade liberalization would destroy an important part of the PRI voting machine over the next decade. This creates a good deal of uncertainty about who will gain lasting power in the future. The Chiapas uprising on January 1, 1994, the day on which NAFTA was enacted, symbolizes this uncertainty. Regardless of whether the uprising originated in the peasantry or was induced by an elite that opposed trade liberalization, it proved that there are opponents to the new regime.[11]

The uncertainty regarding who will get lasting political control once the PRI's agricultural voting machine is weakened will make it politically expedient to delay indefinitely further liberalization or derail reform altogether. My point is that NAFTA is the commitment device that will ensure that such delay will not occur and that reform will continue. This will happen in two ways. First, huge political and economic costs are associated with breaching an international agreement such as NAFTA. Second, NAFTA will consolidate the power of the new export groups that will have in their interest defending the new set of property rights.

NAFTA will benefit and strengthen the new Mexican export elite for two reasons. First, it will facilitate the establishment of links with foreign firms interested in the maintenance of policies that support free trade. Second, it will allow the Mexican export sector to grow and become a big player in the domestic arena. NAFTA will achieve this by reducing the uncertainty generated by trade disputes and by facilitating U.S. and Canadian access to Mexican goods.

---

11. P. Hinestrosa and A. Tornell, "Las Condiciones Economicas Como Factor de Descontento Social: El Caso de Chiapas," in Maria Luisa Armendariz, ed., *Chiapas: Una Radiografia* (Mexico: Fondo de Cultura Economica, 1994).

Also, NAFTA will reduce the cost of inputs, making Mexican exports more competitive. Liberalizing trade in agriculture will increase the supply of unskilled labor, thus reducing the real wages of unskilled workers;[12] liberalizing trade in services will reduce interest rates, transport costs, and communication costs.

By the time the reforms stipulated by NAFTA take effect, the new export groups should have already consolidated their power. Thus, they should be able to defend the new status quo, ensuring that reform is not derailed in the transition. The new groups will be able to defend the new status quo in several ways. For instance, they could finance the campaigns of politicians who favor the status quo as opposed to expropriation and inward-looking policies. Also, should the government in place try to renege on reforms, they could finance opposition groups. Regardless of what parties form and win elections in the future, they will find it costly to alter the development path established by the de la Madrid–Salinas regime. Thus, once the new groups have consolidated their power, the probability of derailment will be small.

The bailout that the Mexican government received in early 1995 after the financial panic of December 1994 exemplifies this point. Given that in early 1995 Mexico did not have enough liquidity to repay its dollar-denominated short-term debt, a default was likely. This default might have forced the government to follow inward-looking policies and increase anew the power of traditional elites, risking the derailment of reforms. The network of U.S. firms with investments in Mexico used its political clout to induce an unprecedentedly speedy response from the U.S. government and international organizations. Within a few weeks approximately fifty billion

12. Anthony Venables and Sweden Van Wijnbergen, *Location Choice, Market Structure, and Barriers to Trade: Foreign Investment and the North American Free Trade Agreement* (London: Centre for Economic Performance, London School of Economics and Political Science, 1993).

dollars in credit lines and loan guarantees was lined up. This support allowed Mexico to repay its short-term debt and even to resume borrowing in international markets by mid-1995. Moreover, the Mexican government responded to this crisis with an acceleration of the privatization program and the opening of the financial system. The fact that the U.S. network used its power to save Mexico from a reform-endangering situation suggests that Salinas was successful in inducing the creation of groups that would defend the reforms begun by de la Madrid.

The Experience of Chile

It is interesting to compare the Chilean and Mexican experiences. The conventional wisdom holds that trade reform took place in Chile because Pinochet was a tough dictator. A closer analysis reveals that causation runs in the opposite direction.[13] Before reform, the powerful groups in Chile were the unions, the import-competing elite, and the landed elite. Unlike Mexico, it was not a drastic collapse in the terms of trade that induced a breakdown of the status quo in Chile but rather a sharp increase in the number of unions. During Frei's administration new rural and urban dwellers' unions were created, and the number of strikes increased dramatically in the late sixties. This trend accelerated during Eduardo Allende's administration, during which many private firms were expropriated. The political change associated with reform was more drastic than that in Mexico. In 1973 a military coup brought Pinochet to power. From my perspective the interesting point is that the

13. See J. Frieden, *Debt, Development, and Democracy* (Princeton, N.J.: Princeton University Press, 1991); A. Valenzuela, *The Breakdown of Democratic Regimes: Chile* (Baltimore, Md.: Johns Hopkins University Press, 1978); A. Velasco, "The State and Economic Policy: Chile 1952–1992," in B. Bosworth, R. Dornbusch, and R. Laban, eds., *The Chilean Economy: Policy Lessons and Challenges* (Washington, D.C.: Brookings Institution, 1994).

trade reform introduced in 1975 destroyed a major part of the man-ufacturing sector but did not generate any opposition from the pri-vate elite or the replacement of Pinochet, as usually has occurred in the rest of Latin America. In fact, Chile was the only case, among the Latin American regimes of the time, that evolved into a personal dictatorship[14] because trade reform destroyed the power of the un-ions. In fact, unionization fell from around 40 percent in 1973 to less than 15 percent in 1990. This point is nicely put by Steppan: "The persistence of fear within the upper bourgeoisie was an im-portant element in the bourgeoisie's willingness to accept individual policies that hurt the upper class . . . but were seen to be the neces-sary cost of protecting its overall interests. It is impossible to under-stand the passivity of the industrial faction of the bourgeoisie in Chile . . . outside of the context of fear."[15]

To summarize a bit, trade reform was an unwanted outcome in Chile and Mexico. It was the costly action undertaken by the private elite to stop the expropriations initiated by its rivals. In both coun-tries powerful groups ended worse off than they had been under the status quo.

Conclusions

In retrospect, the sequence of reform policies adopted in Mexico is fascinating. Neither step resulted from the decree of an all-pow-erful autocrat, and each step both had the support of a powerful group and generated new powerful groups that would support fur-ther reforms. The first step was to liberalize trade in manufactures. The government undertook this action not when it realized its ne-

---

14. S. Huntington, *The Third Wave: Democratization in the Late Twentieth Century* (Norman: University of Oklahoma Press, 1991), chap. 3.

15. A. Steppan, "State Power and the Strength of Civil Society in the Southern Cone of Latin America," in P. Evans, D. Rueschemeyer, and T. Skocpol, eds., *Bringing the State Back In* (Cambridge: Cambridge University Press, 1985), p. 321.

cessity but only when the unanimity of the powerful groups within the manufacturing sector broke down in the 1980s. The second step was to consolidate the power of emerging elites with an interest in export promotion, an objective that the government achieved through privatization and deregulation. The third step in the sequence was the signing of NAFTA, and the fourth step will be to actually dismantle protection in the agriculture and services sectors.

The trade liberalization process was not a historically predetermined outcome but was brought about largely through the decisive contributions of Presidents de la Madrid and Salinas. De la Madrid recognized the window of opportunity created by the economic hardships of the mid-eighties and began liberalization at the start of his administration. He also recognized the limitations of this opportunity and did not try to liberalize the entire economy. Salinas consolidated the power of the new export group and, by signing NAFTA, committed Mexico to total liberalization in fifteen years.

Chances are that if all these steps had been taken at once, Mexico's powerful groups would have colluded and blocked the reform. We can see this from the Venezuelan experience, an interesting contrast to the Mexican one. In 1989–92, Venezuelan president Carlos Andres Perez tried to implement many reforms simultaneously. All the powerful groups in the population opposed him, forcing him to resign. Moreover, his successor, President Caldera, backtracked on many of Perez's reforms.

In Mexico, beginning in the late sixties, it became evident that the protectionist development strategy was no longer beneficial for the country. However, trade liberalization did not take place until 1985, and the badly needed fiscal reform did not take place until 1989. In this chapter, I offer an explanation of why these reforms were delayed and not implemented during the 1970s, when the country could afford the costs associated with these reforms. My premise is that welfare-improving reforms for the country were blocked by powerful interest groups that stand to lose from these reforms.

The interest groups that blocked the reforms during the seventies were the private import-competing elite and the parastatal elite. In the seventies, both groups were interested in keeping the status quo. Since fiscal resources were plentiful, both groups enjoyed high subsidies, which kept the profitability of their fixed assets at a high level. Under these circumstances, it was not profitable for either group to redirect its assets away from productive activities in order to reduce the power of the other group and guarantee for itself a greater share of fiscal revenue. Hence the status quo prevailed.

The equilibrium between these two powerful groups broke down when the debt crisis erupted in 1982 since the government could no longer maintain high levels of subsidies. The struggle between interest groups took place in the spheres of private bank expropriation and trade liberalization. The short-run costs of trade liberalization were the adjustment costs implied by the efficiency effects of free trade. The private elite benefited because the power of the parastatal elite to expropriate and obtain studies was reduced. This mutual weakening gave temporary autonomy to the government to implement fiscal reform.

Index

Adams, John, 91
Africa, 9n
Agency problems, 36, 38
Agricultural sector, 45; Cárdenas government and, 61; protectionism, 142; trade liberalization and, 140–41, 144; trade policy and, 132
Allendé, Salvador, 147
Antipoverty program, 137
Argentina, 79; Australian ballot, 101; homogeneous population, 106; literacy requirements, 100, 105
Army zone commanders, 45
Article 27, Mexican constitution, 43–44, 49, 53, 55
Article 123, Mexican constitution, 43–44, 55; CROM and, 58
Asian economies, 1, 5
Australian ballot, 101
Authoritarianism, 47

Backward integration, 35, 39n15; Mexican policy makers and, 52; organized labor and, 60; political strategy of, 48; postrevolutionary Mexico, 46
Banco de México (Banxico), 51–52

Banco National de México (Banamex), 40, 51
Banking sector, 48–53; credit favoritism and, 4, 138; cronyism in, 1; Díaz government and, 39–40; entry barriers, 50–51; industry-written laws, 50; integration and, 36; Korean, 12–13, 19; nationalization of, 45, 48, 54; nonperforming loans and, 15, 22; parastatal banks, 49; property rights and, 53; statist elite groups and, 138
Bankruptcy, 70, 139
Barbarians-at-the-gates reform model, 129, 131
Beer industry, 70–71
Benefit-cost-analysis, 113–14
Bill of Rights, 47
Bolivia, 100
Brazil, 100; Chamber of Deputies, 110–11, 115–21; economic growth/development, 110, 125; electoral outcomes, 112, 121; imperial period politics, 111–15; party-based voting, 110; political parties in, 109, 110; voting qualifications, 100

Cabrera, Luis, 52

Political Institutions and Economic Growth in Latin America
Essays in Policy, History, and Political Economy

Edited by
Stephen Haber